Penguin Education

Penguin Education Specials
General Editor: Willem van der Eyken

Celebration of Awareness
A Call for Institutional Revolution
ıvan D. Illich

Ivan Illich was born in Vienna in 1926. He studied theology and
philosophy at the Gregorian University in Rome and obtained a
Ph.D. in history at the University of Salzburg. He went to the
United States in 1951, where he served as assistant pastor in an
Irish–Puerto Rican parish in New York City. From 1956 to 1960
he was assigned as vice-rector to the Catholic University of
Puerto Rico, where he organized an intensive training centre
for American priests in Latin American culture. Illich was a
co-founder of the widely known and controversial Center for
Intercultural Documentation (CIDOC) in Cuernavaca, and
since 1964 he has directed research seminars on 'Institutional
Alternatives in a Technological Society', with special focus on
Latin America. His *Deschooling Society*, first published in England
in 1971, is published simultaneously with *Celebration of Awareness*
by Penguin Education.

Celebration of Awareness
A Call for Institutional Revolution
Ivan D. Illich

Introduction by Erich Fromm

Penguin Education

Penguin Education,
A Division of Penguin Books Ltd,
Harmondsworth, Middlesex, England
Penguin Books Australia Ltd,
Ringwood, Victoria, Australia

First published in Great Britain by Calder & Boyars 1971
Published by Penguin Education 1973
Copyright © Ivan D. Illich, 1969, 1970

Made and printed in Great Britain by
Hazell Watson & Viney Ltd,
Aylesbury, Bucks
Set in Monotype Plantin

Contents

Acknowledgements

Portions of this book were first published in the following publications: 'Not Foreigners, yet Foreign' as 'Puerto Ricans in New York: Not Foreigners, yet Foreign', in *Commonweal*, copyright © 1956 by Commonweal Publishing Co. Inc.; 'The Futility of Schooling' in *Saturday Review*, copyright © 1968 by Saturday Review Inc.; 'The Vanishing Clergyman' in the *Critic*, copyright © 1967 by The Thomas More Association; 'The Seamy Side of Charity' as 'To be Perfectly Frank' and 'Violence: A Mirror for Americans' reprinted with permission from *America*, 21 January 1967, and 27 April 1968, all rights reserved, copyright © 1967, 1968 by America Press Inc., 106 West 56th Street, New York, NY, 10019; 'School: The Sacred Cow' as 'Commencement At the University of Puerto Rico' and 'Planned Poverty: The End Result of Technical Assistance' as 'Outwitting the "Developed" Countries' in the *New York Review of Books*; 'A Constitution for Cultural Revolution' as 'The Need for Cultural Revolution' in 'Great Books Today' 1970, copyright © 1970 by Encyclopaedia Britannica Inc.

Introduction

There is no need for an introduction of the following papers or of their author. If, nevertheless, Dr Illich has honoured me by the invitation to write such an introduction, and if I gladly accepted, the reason in both our minds seems to be that this introduction offers an occasion that permits clarifying the nature of a common attitude and faith, in spite of the fact that some of our views differ considerably. Even the author's own views today are not always the same as those he held at the time he wrote these papers, on different occasions, over the course of the years. But he has remained true to himself in the very core of his approach and it is this core that we share.

It is not easy to find the proper word to describe this core. How can a fundamental approach to life be caught in a concept without distorting and twisting it? Yet since we need to communicate with words, the most adequate – or rather, the least inadequate – term seems to be 'humanist radicalism'.

What is meant by radicalism? What does *humanist* radicalism imply?

By radicalism I do not refer primarily to a certain set of ideas, but rather to an attitude, to an 'approach', as it were. To begin with this approach can be characterized by the motto: *de omnibus dubitandum*; everything must be doubted, particularly the ideological concepts which are virtually shared by everybody and have consequently assumed the role of indubitable common-sensical axioms.

To 'doubt' in this sense does not imply a psychological state of inability to arrive at decisions or convictions, as is the case in obsessional doubt, but the readiness and capacity for critical questioning of all assumptions and institutions which have become idols under the name of common sense, logic, and what is supposed to be 'natural'. This radical questioning is possible only if one does not take the concepts of one's own society or even of an entire historical period – like Western culture since the Renaissance – for granted, and furthermore if one enlarges the scope of one's awareness and penetrates into the unconscious aspects of one's thinking. Radical doubt is an act of uncovering and discovering; it is the dawning of the awareness that the Emperor is naked, and that his splendid garments are nothing but the product of one's fantasy.

Radical doubt means to question; it does not necessarily mean to negate. It is easy to negate by simply positing the opposite of what exists; radical doubt is dialectical in as much as it comprehends the process of the unfolding of oppositions and aims at a new synthesis which negates *and* affirms.

Radical doubt is a process; a process of liberation from idolatrous thinking; a widening of awareness, of imaginative, creative vision of our possibilities and options. The radical approach does not occur in a vacuum. It does not start from nothing, but it starts from the roots, and the root, as Marx once said, is man. But to say 'the root is man' is not meant in a positivistic, descriptive sense. When we speak of man we speak of him not as a thing but as a process; we speak of his potential for developing all his powers; those for greater intensity of being, greater harmony, greater love, greater awareness. We also speak of man with a potential to be corrupted, of his power *to* act being transformed into the passion for power *over* others, of his love of life degenerating into the passion to destroy life.

Humanistic radicalism is radical questioning guided by insight into the dynamics of man's nature; and by concern for man's growth and full unfolding. In contrast to contemporary positivistic thinking it is not 'objective', if objectivity means theorizing without a passionately held aim which impels and nourishes the process of thinking. But it is exceedingly objective if it means that every step in the process of thinking is based on critically sifted evidence, and furthermore if it takes a critical attitude towards common-sensical premises. All this means that humanist radicalism questions every idea and every institution from the standpoint of whether it helps or hinders man's capacity for greater aliveness and joy. This is not the place to give lengthy examples for the kind of common-sensical premises that are questioned by humanist radicalism. It is not necessary to do so either, since Dr Illich's papers deal precisely with such examples as the usefulness of compulsive schooling, or of the present function of priests. Many more could be added, some of which are implied in the author's papers. I want to mention only a few like the modern concept of 'progress', which means the principle of ever-increasing production, consumption, timesaving, maximal efficiency and profit, and calculability of all economic activities without regard to their effect on the quality of living and the unfolding of man; or the dogma that increasing consumption makes man happy, that the management of large-scale enterprises must necessarily be bureaucratic and alienated; that the aim of life is having (and using), not being; that reason resides in the intellect and is split from the affective life; that the newer is always better than the older; that radicalism is the negation of tradition; that the opposite of 'law and order' is lack of structure. In short, that the ideas and categories that have arisen during the development of modern science and industrialism are superior to those of all former cultures and indispensable for the progress of the human race.

Humanistic radicalism questions all these premises and is not afraid of arriving at ideas and solutions that may sound absurd. I see the great value in the writings of Dr Illich precisely in the fact that they represent humanistic radicalism in its fullest and most imaginative aspect. The author is a man of rare courage, great aliveness, extraordinary erudition and brilliance, and fertile imaginativeness, whose whole thinking is based on his concern for man's unfolding – physically, spiritually and intellectually. The importance of his thoughts in this as well as his other writings lies in the fact that they have a liberating effect on the mind by showing entirely new possibilities; they make the reader more alive because they open the door that leads out of the prison of routinized, sterile, preconceived notions. By the creative shock they communicate – except to those who react only with anger at so much nonsense – they help to stimulate energy and hope for a new beginning.

Erich Fromm

Foreword

Each chapter in this volume records an effort of mine to question the nature of some certainty. Each therefore deals with deception – the deception embodied in one of our institutions. Institutions create certainties, and taken seriously, certainties deaden the heart and shackle the imagination. It is always my hope that my statements, angry or passionate, artful or innocent, will also provoke a smile, and thus a new freedom – even though the freedom come at a cost.

Shortly after original publication most of these papers became notorious. This was not accident. Each essay was written in a different language, addressed to a different group of believers, meant to hit home at a particular crisis of confidence. Each rubbed some well-established bureaucrats the wrong way, at the moment the latter were finding it difficult to rationalize a 'business as usual' position.

These pieces were, therefore, literally written for the moment. The passage of time since some of them appeared has qualified an occasional detail: statistics, or the situation discussed – even my own attitude – may have altered since, in some manner or degree. But I have purposely not, in the journalistic phrase, 'updated' the articles for presentation in this book form. They constitute a point of view on a phenomenon of a time, and should stand thus. Their compilation has also inevitably resulted in some repetitive statements of fact and some duplications of expressions. These too I leave as stated, for emphasis and for the record – though I would have avoided them had I thought originally that one day I would gather my occasional writings under one cover.

1 A Call to Celebration

This 'call to celebration' was a manifesto jointly enunciated by and reflecting the mood of a group of friends in 1967, among them Robert Fox and Robert Theobald. It was written at the time of the March on the Pentagon. This call to face facts, rather than deal in illusions – to live change, rather than rely on engineering – is an attempt to re-introduce the word 'celebration' into ordinary English.

I and many others, known and unknown to me, call upon you:

To celebrate our joint power to provide all human beings with the food, clothing and shelter they need to delight in living.

To discover, together with us, what we must do to use mankind's power to create the humanity, the dignity and the joyfulness of each one of us.

To be responsibly aware of your personal ability to express your true feelings and to gather us together in their expression.

We can only live these changes: we cannot think our way to humanity. Every one of us, and every group with which we live and work, must become the model of the era which we desire to create. The many models which will develop should give each one of us an environment in which we can celebrate our potential – and discover the way into a more humane world.

We are challenged to break the obsolete social and economic systems which divide our world between the overprivileged and the underprivileged. All of us, whether governmental leader or protester, businessman or worker, professor or student share a common guilt. We have failed to discover how the necessary changes in our ideals and our social structures can be made. Each of us, therefore, through our ineffectiveness and our lack of responsible awareness, causes the suffering around the world.

All of us are crippled – some physically, some mentally, some emotionally. We must therefore strive cooperatively to create the new world. There is no time left for destruction, for hatred, for anger. We must build, in hope and joy and celebration. Let us meet the new era of abundance with self-chosen work and freedom to follow the drum of one's own heart. Let us recognize that a striving for self-realization, for poetry and play, is basic to man once his needs for food, clothing and shelter have been met – that we will choose those areas of activity which will contribute to our own development and will be meaningful to our society.

But we must also recognize that our thrust toward self-realization is profoundly hampered by outmoded, industrial-age structures. We are presently constrained and driven by the impact of man's ever growing powers. Our existing systems force us to develop and accept any weaponry system which may be technologically possible; our present systems force us to develop and accept any improvement in machinery, equipment, materials and supplies which will increase production and lower costs; our present systems force us to develop and accept advertising and consumer seduction.

In order to persuade the citizen that he controls his destiny, that morality informs decisions, and that technology is the servant rather than the driving force, it is necessary today to distort information. The ideal of informing the public has given way to trying to convince the public that forced actions are actually desirable actions.

Miscalculations in these increasingly complex rationalizations and consequent scandal, account for the increasing preoccupation with the honesty of both private and public decision makers. It is therefore tempting to attack those holding roles such as national leader, administrator, manager, executive, labour leader, professor, student, parent. But such attacks on individuals often disguise the real nature of the crisis we confront: the demonic nature of present systems which force man to consent to his own deepening self-destruction.

We can escape from these dehumanizing systems. The way ahead will be found by those who are unwilling to be constrained by the apparently all-determining forces and structures of the industrial age. Our freedom and power are determined by our willingness to accept responsibility for the future.

Indeed the future has already broken into the present. We each live in many times. The present of one is the past of another, and the future of yet another. We are called to live, knowing and showing that the future exists and that each one of us can call it in, when we are willing, to redress the balance of the past.

In the future we must end the use of coercive power and authority: the ability to demand action on the basis of one's hierarchical position. If any one phrase can sum up the nature of the new era, it is *the end of privilege and licence*.

We must abandon our attempt to solve our problems through shifting power balances or attempting to create more efficient bureaucratic machines.

We call you to join man's race to maturity, to work with us in inventing the future. We believe that a human adventure is just beginning: that mankind has so far been restricted in developing its innovative and creative powers because it was overwhelmed by toil. Now we are free to be as human as we will.

The celebration of man's humanity through joining together in the healing expression of one's relationships with others, and one's growing acceptance of one's own nature and needs, will clearly create major confrontations with existing values and systems. The expanding dignity of each man and each human relationship must necessarily challenge existing systems.

The call is to live the future. Let us join together joyfully to celebrate our awareness that we can make our life today the shape of tomorrow's future.

2 Violence: A Mirror for Americans

The compulsion to do good is an innate American trait. Only North Americans seem to believe that they always should, may, and actually can choose somebody with whom to share their blessings. Ultimately this attitude leads to bombing people into the acceptance of gifts.

In early 1968 I tried with insistence to make some of my friends understand this image of the American overseas. I was speaking mainly to resisters engaged in organizing the march on the Pentagon. I wanted to share with them a profound fear: the fear that the end of the war in Vietnam would permit hawks and doves to unite in a destructive war on poverty in the Third World.

The qualified failure of the war on poverty, with its fruits of urban riots, has begun to open the eyes of Americans to the reasons for the failure of the Alliance for Progress, with its fruits of threatened rebellion. Both are related to the failure to win the hearts and minds of the people of Asia by an outpouring of money and human lives that Americans perceive as an expression of heroic generosity, in the defence of South Vietnam. Failure in Harlem, Guatemala and Vietnam has a common root. All three have miscarried because the United States gospel of massive material achievement lacks credibility for the world's overwhelming majorities. I believe that insight into the meaning of United States good will as perceived by Latin Americans or Asians would enable Americans to perceive the meaning of the problem of their own slums; it could even lead to the perception of a new and more effective policy.

I have had the opportunity to observe this growing awareness of a common root of failure in my contacts with students at Cuernavaca. There, at the Center for Intercultural Documentation, for the past two years we have offered a sequence of workshops to compare the experience of poverty in capital-rich and capital-starved societies. We have witnessed the initial shock in many Americans dedicated to the war against poverty, when they observed and studied Latin America and realized for the first time that there is a link between minority marginality at home and mass margination overseas. Their emotional reaction is usually more acute than the intellectual insight that produces it. We have seen more than one man lose his balance as he suddenly lost the faith that for him had previously supported that balance, the faith that says: 'The American way is the solution for all.' For any good man, whether he is a social worker in Watts or a missionary on his way to Bolivia, it means pain and panic to realize that he is seen by 90 per cent of mankind as the exploiting outsider who shores up his privilege by promoting a delusive belief in the ideals of democracy, equal opportunity and free enterprise among people who haven't a remote possibility of profiting from them.

At this stage of the war in Vietnam the violent symptoms are too horrible to permit a lucid analysis of the causes that produce them. It is therefore more important to focus United States attention on the other two programmes, the war on poverty and the Alliance for Progress: one, a war conducted by social workers; the other, an alliance that has maintained or swept into power military regimes in two-thirds of the Latin American countries. Both originated in the name of good will; both are now seen as pacification programmes; both are pregnant with violence.

The war on poverty aims at the integration of the so-called underprivileged minorities of the United States into the mainstream of the American way of life; the Alliance for Progress aims at the integration of the so-called underdeveloped countries of Latin America into the community of industrialized nations. Both programmes were designed to have the poor join the American dream. Both programmes failed. The poor refused to dream on command. The order to dream and the money they got only made them rambunctious. Huge funds were appropriated to start the United States minorities and the Latin American majorities on the way of integration into a United States-style middle class: the world of college attendance, universal consumer credit, the world of household appliances and insurance, the world of church and movie attendance. An army of generous volunteers swarmed through New York ghettos and Latin American jungle canyons, pushing the persuasion that makes America tick.

The frustrated social worker and the former Peace Corps volunteer are now among the few who explain to mainline America that the poor are right in rejecting forced conversion to the American gospel. Only seven years after the majority missionary enterprise of the Alliance was launched, riot squads at home, military governments in Latin America and the army in Vietnam keep asking for more funds. But now it can be seen that the money is needed not for the uplift of the poor, but to protect the frail beachhead into the middle class that has been gained by the few converts who have benefited here or there by the American way of life.

Comparison of these three theatres of United States missionary effort and war will help bring home a truism: the American society of achievers and consumers, with its two-party system and its universal schooling, perhaps befits those who have got it, but certainly not the rest of the world. A 15 per cent minority at home who earn less than $3000 a year, and an 80 per cent majority abroad who earn less than $300 a year are prone to react with violence to the schemes by which they are fitted into coexistence with affluence. This is the moment to bring home to the people of the United States the fact that the way of life they have chosen is not viable enough to be shared. Eight years ago I told the late Bishop Manuel Larrain, the president of the Conference of Latin American Bishops, that I was prepared if necessary to dedicate my efforts to stop the coming of missionaries to Latin America. His answer still rings in my ears: 'They may be useless to us in Latin America, but they are the only North Americans whom we will have the opportunity to educate. We owe them that much.'

At this moment, when neither the allure of money nor the power of persuasion nor control through weapons can efface the prospect of violence, during the summer in the slums and throughout the year in Guatemala, Bolivia or Venezuela, we can analyse the analogies in the reactions to United States policy in the three main theatres of its defensive war: the war by which it defends its quasi-religious persuasion in Watts, Latin America and Vietnam. Fundamentally this is the same war fought on three fronts; it is the war to 'preserve the values of the West'. Its origin and expression are associated with generous motives and a high ideal to provide a richer life for all men. But as the threatening implications of that ideal begin to emerge, the enterprise grinds down to one compelling purpose: to protect the style of life and the style of death that affluence makes possible for a very few; and since that style cannot be protected without being expanded, the affluent declare it obligatory for all. 'That they may have more' begins to be seen in its real perspective: 'That I may not have less'.

In all three theatres of war the same strategies are used: money, troopers, teachers. But money can benefit only a few in the ghettos, and a few in Latin America, and a few in Vietnam; and the consequent concentration of imported benefits on a few requires their ever tighter protection against the many. For the majority of marginal people, the economic growth of their surroundings means rising levels of frustration. On all three frontiers of affluence, therefore, the gun becomes important to protect the achiever. Police reinforcements go hand in hand with bands of armed citizens in the United States. In Guatemala the recently murdered military attaché of the United States had just admitted that the American Embassy had to assist in arming right-wing goon squads because they are more efficient in maintaining order (and certainly more cruel) than the army.

Next to money and guns, the United States idealist turns up in every theatre of the war; the teacher, the volunteer, the missionary, the community organizer, the economic developer. Such men define their role as service. Actually they frequently wind up numbing the damage done by money and weapons, or seducing the 'underdeveloped' to the benefits of the world of affluence and achievement. They especially are the ones for whom 'ingratitude' is the bitter reward. They are the personifications of Good Old Charlie Brown: 'How can you lose when you are so sincere?'

I submit that, if present trends continue, from now on the violence in Harlem, in Latin America, in Asia, will increasingly be directed against the foreign and native 'persuasion pusher' of this kind. Increasingly the 'poor' will slam the door in the face of salesmen for the United States system of politics, education and economics as an answer to their needs. This rejection goes hand in hand with a growing loss of faith in his own tenets on the part of the salesman of United States social consensus. Disaffection, helplessness and the response of anger at the United States have undermined the thrust of the formerly guileless enthusiast of the American way and American methods.

I submit that foreign gods (ideals, idols, ideologies, persuasions, values) are more offensive to the 'poor' than the military or economic power of the foreigner. It is more irritating to feel seduced to the consumption of overpriced sugar-water called Coca-Cola than to submit helplessly to doing the same job an American does, only at half the pay. It angers a person more to hear a priest preach cleanliness, thrift, resistance to socialism or obedience to unjust authority, than to accept military rule. If I read present trends correctly, and I am confident I do, during the next few years violence will break out mostly against symbols of foreign ideas and the attempt to sell these. And I fear that this violence, which is fundamentally a healthy though angry and turbulent rejection of alienating symbols, will be exploited and will harden into hatred and crime. The recent violence in Detroit, Washington and Cincinnati after the murder of Martin Luther King shows how the impatience of the ghetto dwellers in the United States can erupt into violence and vandalism at the slightest spark.

Violence, therefore, covers a broad spectrum of experience: from the explosion of frustrated vitality to the fanatical rejection of alienating idols. It is important to stress this distinction. But as United States thinkers are horrified by the heartless slaughter in Vietnam, and fascinated by the inability of a white majority to suppress the life of a people, it is not easy to keep the distinction clear. The emotional involvement of the average United States student with Vietnam and the ghettos is so deep, it is almost taboo to call his attention to the distinction. For this reason we must welcome any educational effort that allows United States students to perceive reactions to the United States way of life in the third theatre of the war against poverty: Latin America.

In the mirror of Latin America, violence in American ghettos and on the borders of China can be seen in its new meaning, as a rejection of American values. From experience of years in Cuernavaca, dealing with United States 'idea salesmen', I know this insight is costly to come by. There is no exit from a way of life built on $5000-plus per year, and there is no possible road leading into this way of life for nine out of ten men in our generation and the next. And for the nine it is revolting to hear a message of economic and social salvation presented by the affluent that, however, sincerely expressed, leads the 'poor' to believe that it is their fault that they do not fit into God's world as it should be and as it has been decreed that it should be around the North Atlantic.

It is not the American way of life lived by a handful of millions that sickens the thousands of millions, but rather the growing awareness that those who live the American way will not tire until the superiority of their quasi-religious persuasion is accepted by the underdogs. Living violence always breaks out against the demand that a man submit to idols. Planned violence is then promoted as justified by the need to reduce a man or a people to the service of the idol they threaten to reject. Francisco Juliao, the peasant leader from North-east Brazil who now lives in exile in Cuernavaca, recently made a statement that clarifies these principles. 'Never,' he said, 'but never put weapons into the hands of the people. Whosoever puts weapons into the hands of the people destroys. Weapons put into the hands of the people will always be used against them. Weapons always defeat the poor who receive them. Only the brick and the stick a man picks up in anger will not defile him as a man.'

In this light it is important for the North American citizen to learn from the insight gained these years by Latin American thinkers. Let him look at Colombia where there are bandits who kill for gain, and soldiers and *guerrilleros* who kill each other for the sake of discipline or in the service of a flag; and there is the angry man who kills in a mob that erupts in riot; and finally there is the witness, like Camilo Torres, who purposefully withdraws to the mountains to demonstrate his ability to survive in the face of an oppressive regime and thus wants to prove its illegitimacy. Soldier and bandit can organize; riots can be incited and their frustrated vitality can go stale or be channelled with deadly rationality into the service of some 'ideal'. Testimony will always remain a lonely task that ends up on a hill like Calvary. True testimony of profound non-conformity arouses the fiercest violence against it, but I do not see how such witness could ever be organized or institutionalized.

The study of violence in Latin America deeply touches the life of the United States observer, but – for a moment still – allows him to stay disengaged. It is always easier to see the illusions in one's neighbour's eyes than the delusions in one's own. A critical examination of the effect that intense social change has on the intimacy of the human heart in Latin America is a fruitful way to insight into the intimacy of the human heart in the United States. In the capital-starved economies of Latin America, a great majority live excluded, now and forever, from the benefits of a thriving United States-style elite middle class. In the immensely rich economy of the United States, a small minority clamours that, in the same way, it is excluded from the mass of the middle class. The comparison should enable the United States observer to understand the world-wide growth of two societies, separate and unequal, and to appreciate the dynamics that provoke violence between them.

3 Not Foreigners, yet Foreign

From 1951 to 1956 I lived as a priest in Incarnation Parish on the West Side of New York's Manhattan. Puerto Ricans were then being crowded into the walk-ups between Amsterdam Avenue and Broadway. They were displacing many families who had moved a generation earlier straight from Ireland to this area. I became involved in the inevitable conflict between these peoples and also in the controversy about its meaning.

As a newcomer to the United States I was surprised to see how New Yorkers, from druggist to mayor, fell back upon ready stereotypes to guide their policy decisions. Whatever was worth understanding about Puerto Ricans, they apparently felt, could be explained in old categorical terms coined for preceding groups of immigrants. That which had served for the Poles or Italians should fit the Puerto Ricans.

At that time I tried to obtain recognition of the fact that, at least for the Roman Catholic Church, the Puerto Rican immigration represented a phenomenon without precedent. Amazingly, I found an inquisitive listener to my opinion in Cardinal Spellman.

After the introduction of the quota system in 1924, it seemed that the melting process in New York City was finally about to catch up with the number of people tossed into the pot. Then in the late 1940s, the city was presented with a novel challenge, an invasion of American-born 'foreigners', the Puerto Ricans. In Vito Marcantonio's heyday (1943) there were less than thirty-five thousand Puerto Ricans in New York; at present (1956) there are more than half a million, and indications are that the migration has not yet reached its peak.

These Puerto Ricans are not foreigners, and yet they are more foreign than most of the immigrants who preceded them. About this seeming paradox the well-meaning should be well-informed, since to be received kindly merely because one is a foreigner is a cold kind of condescension: the chances are that the man who thus receives you is determined never really to know you.

If on the one hand a man consistently designates you a foreigner, he usually precludes any possibility of appreciating that which is unique to your group – besides the fact that it is not his own. If on the other hand, misunderstanding St Paul's instruction to make himself Jew with the Jews and Greek with the Greeks, he approaches you with an exegesis such as 'We are all Americans', he denies your right, and his, to a heritage, to be human, with roots reaching back in history.

This fallacy is at the bottom of the attitude of many well-meaning people toward the Puerto Rican immigrants: let them do what the Irish or Italians did, or let them attempt what the Jews attempted; let them grow gradually through their own national parishes, territorial ghettos and political machines to full 'Americanization'; let them vociferously assert that they are as good Americans as the man next door. These attitudes are very common in New York, where the arrival of successive migratory waves is taken for granted. It is too often gratuitously assumed that the future novel about the Puerto Rican journey will be fashioned after either *The Last Hurrah* or *Marjorie Morning-Star*, or will be a combination of both.

The welfare investigator who says to José Rivera, 'My parents went through the same experience,' neither lies nor expresses xenophobia – he just misunderstands, like the politician who tries again to use methods which worked when Italian was spoken in Harlem.

When the Irish and the Germans came here a century ago, New York City was faced with a challenge of a kind never experienced before and of a size never to be duplicated. In 1855 one-third of the city's population (500,000) consisted of immigrants who had arrived in the previous decade; against this proportion the one-fifteenth of the city's population which in 1955 consisted of recently arrived Puerto Ricans (again 500,000) seems insignificant.

In the days of the heavy influx to America, wave after wave of immigrants arrived, settled, and became accustomed to new patterns of life. The newcomers spoke different languages, worshipped in different churches, came from different climates, wooed in different fashions, ate different dishes, sang different songs. But under these apparent differences they had much in common. They came from the Old Continent and arrived as refugees or settlers to become Americans and to stay for good. They brought their own clergy – rabbi, priest or minister – and the symbols of past millennia which were their own, St Patrick, the Mafia or Loretto, no less than the Turnverein. They settled in special sections of the city and kept to themselves for years before they ventured to take part in that experience new to all of them: life in a pluralistic society. They fell into a common pattern, and it is no wonder that those who had been here long enough to consider themselves part of a settled stratum fell into the habit of assuming a priori that each new incoming group would be analogous to theirs. This assumption, in fact, proved to be true until after the Second World War, with the exception of two groups, the Orientals and the Southern Negroes.

Then suddenly the Puerto Ricans arrived *en masse*. New York had never before known such an invasion, an invasion of Americans who came from an older part of the New World into New York, which, by the way, had been part of the diocese of San Juan long before Henry Hudson discovered Manhattan. And New York had never had to deal with American-born citizens who in their schools had learned English as a foreign language.

These strange Americans were sons of a Catholic country where for centuries slaves had found refuge, where the population of a little over two million is overwhelmingly white but where a difference in the shade of the skin is no impediment, either to success or to marriage. Yet theirs was the first sizeable group coming from overseas into New York to be tagged by many as 'coloured', much less because of the racial heredity of some than for the vaguely sensed great difference between them and former new arrivals.

This was a new type of immigrant: not a European who had left home for good and strove to become an American, but an American citizen, who could come here for the time between one harvest and another and return home for vacation with a week's salary spent on an air-coach ticket. This was not the fugitive from racial or religious persecution in his own country, but the child of 'natives' in a Spanish colony or perhaps the descendant of a Spanish official in the colonial service; not a man accustomed to be led by men of his own stock – priest, politician, rebel or professor – but for four hundred years a subject in a territory administered by foreigners, first Spanish, then American, only recently come into its own.

The new arrival from Puerto Rico was not the Christian in his own right who received the Faith from the sons of his own neighbours, but the fruit of missionary labour typical of the Spanish Empire. He was a Catholic, born of parents who were also Catholics, yet he received the Sacraments from a foreigner because the government was afraid that to train native priests might be to train political rebels.

Even the physical configuration of the world from which he came was different. He was a man from an island where nature is provident and a friend, where field labour means much more harvesting than planting. When nature rebels every few decades, he is powerless; in the hurricanes he cannot but see the finger of God.

Until recently nobody in Puerto Rico built a house with the idea that it should survive the elements or withstand the climate by air conditioning. What a difference from the Pole and the Sicilian, both of whom built houses to withstand nature, climate and time, both of whom built houses to separate their lives from that of nature. One might have come from the Russian steppe or the ghetto and the other from an olive grove on the coast but both knew what winter meant; they knew that a house was there to protect them from the cold, a place within which to make a home. It was easy for the Pole and the Sicilian to settle in tenements and to live confined there. But the new immigrant from the tropics knew no winter, and the home he left was a hut *in* which you slept but *around* which you lived with your family. The hut was the centre of his day's activities, not their limit. To come to a tenement, to need heat, to need glass in your windows, to be frowned on for tending to live beyond your doors – this was all contrary to the Puerto Rican's traditional habits, and as surprising to him as it is for the New Yorker to realize that for any immigrants these basic assumptions of his life should be surprising.

The new Puerto Rico, the Puerto Rico of 1956, is studded with concrete houses and opens a new factory every day. It is a proving ground for the most advanced forms of community organizations, and it has the fastest-declining rate for illiteracy and the fastest-falling mortality in the world. Yet these facts must not make us think that the traditional outlook of its people has changed or will change tomorrow. These material improvements are the outcome of the first decade of Múñoz Marín's administration, but they do not wipe out the Island's past nor are they intended to make of San Juan a suburb of New York.

The differences between the Puerto Rican migration and the influx of Europeans are fundamental. Indeed, in the shortness of its history Puerto Rico is more foreign to Europe than to America. These differences account for much of the distinctive behaviour characteristics of Puerto Ricans in New York, and the lack of knowledge of these differences accounts for many misunderstandings on the part of old New Yorkers.

Many a Puerto Rican does not leave the Island with a clear plan of settling on the mainland. How can a man who leaves on the spur of the moment, planning to make a fast dollar in New York and be back as soon as he has enough to buy a store, take roots in New York? I remember one woman who was in despair because her husband had disappeared on his way to the cane fields, carrying his machete. She thought, of course, that a rival had grabbed him from her. And then, after a week, she got a money order from Chicago. On the way to the cane field he had run into a hiring gang and decided to try his luck – and that was the reason he neglected to come home for dinner. In a case like this, in which a man 'drops in' on New York, with no intentions of staying but of eventually commuting 'home', how can the transient have the same effect on his neighbourhood in New York as the old immigrant who came to stay? Yet the statistical curve of emigration from the Island is in exact correlation with the curve of employment on the mainland. If employment is scarce, the reflux increases correspondingly. Many, even after years in New York, feel they got stuck there because of money.

With the arrival of hundreds of thousands from Puerto Rico and the other Central American states (it is estimated that more than one-quarter of New York's Spanish–American population is not Puerto Rican), not only a new language but a new pattern of living has been added to the city. Instead of the strangers speaking only a foreign tongue who formerly arrived exhausted from the long journey, American citizens, all of whom know some basic English, arrive in aeroplanes within six hours of leaving their tropical island.

The old immigrants settled in national neighbourhoods; the new transatlantic commuter spreads out all over the city; ten years after the beginning of the Puerto Rican mass influx Spanish has already become ubiquitous in New York. Unlike European immigrants, all Puerto Ricans know some English, and this helped, but there is another factor that has contributed to Latin Americans spreading to all quarters of the city. In former times when a neighbourhood became a centre for the newest immigrant group, it was either a slum or tended to become one. And once a neighbourhood had deteriorated it hardly ever was redeemed. The great immigration from Puerto Rico started after the Second World War, due to such factors as cheap air transportation, acquaintance with the mainland acquired by many during service in the army, rising education under the new political order on the island, and, last but not least, the growing pressure of a population which has more than doubled since the beginning of the century. At that same time the city was embarking on its great slum clearance programme and the first blocks to be torn down were almost invariably those where the newest and poorest immigrant had just settled. As a result, the Puerto Ricans began to be resettled all around town in new projects and on a non-discriminatory basis.

Considering this dispersal and the tendency to commute to the Island, it is no wonder that there are hardly any Puerto Rican national neighbourhoods in the traditional sense in New York. One result is that it is difficult for Puerto Ricans to develop local grass-roots leadership within their own group; either their concentration per city block is too thin, or the intention to stick to the neighbourhood is absent, or the necessity to organize in association with their own is weak because all are citizens who at least understand some English and have official 'protection' from the Commonwealth government labour office – the first instance of something like a 'Consulate for American Nationals'. And there is no doubt that another factor contributing to the relative lack of leadership is caused by hundreds of years of colonial administration.

Thus Puerto Ricans in New York find it more difficult than groups which came before them to form their own in-group leadership, if they do not find it completely impossible. This fact gives them a very real advantage over former migrations in one sense, because it almost forces them into an active participation in the established community. On the other hand, the sudden challenge of having to participate in a settled New York community proves too arduous for many who might have been able to become leaders in their own cliques.

A lack of consideration on the part of New York civic leaders for the distinctive character of this new Puerto Rican migration, as compared to previous immigrant experiences, can do real damage to the community by either retarding or injuring the new pattern of assimilation which will have to form. If this lack of understanding should be present in the leaders of the Catholic Church, it can seriously damage souls.

One-third of the baptized Catholics in Manhattan and the lower Bronx are Spanish–Americans at this moment. The Puerto Ricans are the first group of Catholics with a distinctly non-European tradition of Catholicism to come to the East Coast. The lack of native priests, due to the colonial and imperialistic atmosphere of more than four hundred years of the Island's history, and also the special approaches due to missionary conditions, have profoundly moulded the behaviour of Puerto Ricans as Catholics.

Notwithstanding the very recent trend toward rapid urbanization, the majority of Puerto Ricans are dispersed over the steep hills of the interior, living in huts in the midst of small clearings among bananas and flamboyants, with magnificent views, but too far from church to attend Mass every Sunday. Traditionally, they take the Sacraments on those rare occasions when the priest comes to visit them in the chapel in their barrio – but for generations they have had to baptize their own children because the priest came so seldom. Under such circumstances regular attendance at Sunday Mass is not a confirmed element of Catholic practice. Living habits of the tropics, feudal-colonial social organization, and the confluence of Indian, African and European cultures played their part. The Church's law declaring a marriage between two Catholics valid even when not entered into before a priest, if a priest could not be available in less than a month, made people forget the need for a priest. It had an adverse effect on the frequency of marriages in church, and still has today.

'Bad habits' like these are not a sign of lack of Catholic spirit, but rather the effects of a peculiar ecclesiastical history. Many United States Catholics are used to a wide variety of national customs in national parishes and a great difference in practices among various ethnic groups; when faced with the lack of 'practice' of their faith by Puerto Ricans, they might be tempted to identify them with some other foreign group in whom the effects of a different background show up in similar behaviour, or might even deny altogether that Puerto Ricans are Catholic. But for anybody who has ever breathed the atmosphere of the Island there is no doubt that theirs is a Catholic folk-culture: children who might never make their First Communion will regularly ask their parents' blessing before leaving the house; people who might never have been taught the catechism will devoutly invoke the names of Our Lord or the Virgin and plaster their homes with holy pictures and sign themselves with the Cross before leaving home. Even the fact that a man refuses to get married in church sometimes testifies for rather than against his Catholicity; he does not want to bind himself forever by a Church marriage.

In Puerto Rico God's house extends from the church into the

plaza. Not only do the processions or posedas require the out-of-doors as a continuation of the church, but also the church is often too small, and throngs attend Mass by looking through doors and windows. Unless his neighbour on the mainland understands the different meaning 'family', 'church' or 'home' has for a man from the tropics, he will not understand why José plays the guitar on his doorstep, or why María walks from statue to statue during Mass for a little chat with the saints or perhaps enters church only after service, because she is repelled by the formality of the ushers.

All of this points towards the need the Puerto Ricans have to win some respect for their background. What they need is not more help but less categorization according to previous schemes, and more understanding. Only thus will they be able to make the unique cultural, political and economic contribution for which they seem destined: Spanish–Christian tradition, a Catholicism in which is taken for granted an eminently Christian attitude towards the mixing of races, a freshness and simplicity of outlook proper to the tropics, a new pattern of political freedom in association with the United States, a bridge between the hemispheres politically and culturally no less than economically – these are only a few of the assets that the mass migration of Puerto Ricans to the mainland can contribute to New York and the United States.

4 The Eloquence of Silence

Five years on the streets of New York made me aware of the
need for some method of bringing native New Yorkers to
friendship with Puerto Ricans. Ministers, teachers, social
workers, all were submerged in a Spanish-speaking crowd.
They needed to learn the language, but even more they
needed to attune their ears and open their hearts to the
anguish of a people who were lonely, frightened and powerless.

Quite evidently the mere study of Spanish was not enough.
The man who can construct sentences with words and
grammar may be much further from reality than he who
knows that he does not speak a language. I saw how intensely
Puerto Ricans rejected the Americano who studied them for
the purpose of 'integrating them' in the city. They even
refused to answer in Spanish, because behind his benevolence
they sensed the condescension and often the contempt.
A programme was needed to help native New Yorkers to
enter into the spirit of poverty.

In 1956 I became Vice-Rector of the Catholic University
of Puerto Rico and this gave me a chance to prepare people
for work in the Spanish ghettos. We offered workshops
combining the very intensive study of spoken Spanish with
field experience and with the academic study of Puerto
Rican poetry, history, songs and social reality. Many of my
students came at great personal sacrifice. More than half
were priests, mostly below the age of thirty-five. They had
decided to spend their lives among the poor in the inner city.
It is now difficult to remember how the Catholic clergy then
felt about its duty. It was hard to convince an Irish–
American pastor to permit his curate to spend his time on
people who never came to church. The Spanish language was
a potent tool for curates who wanted to use their time and

the resources of the Church for work among the poor.
Because – presumably – the Spanish language identified those
poor who were born Catholics, and to whom the Church
under no circumstances could deny an equal share of its
ministry. When seven years later the war on poverty broke
out, a substantial number of recognized leaders and critics
were these men who had met each other in Puerto Rico.
With this group of students I could explore the deeper
meaning involved in the learning of a foreign language.
In fact, I believe that properly conducted language learning is
one of the few occasions in which an adult can go through a
deep experience of poverty, of weakness, and of dependence
on the good will of another. Every evening we gathered for
an hour of silent prayer. At the beginning of the hour one of
us would offer points for meditation. The following is one of
the sessions recorded by a participant.

The science of linguistics has brought into view new horizons in the understanding of human communications. An objective study of the ways in which meanings are transmitted has shown that much more is relayed from one man to another through and in silence than in words. Words and sentences are composed of silences more meaningful than the sounds. The pregnant pauses between sounds and utterances become luminous points in an incredible void: as electrons in the atom, as planets in the solar system. Language is as a cord of silence with sounds the knots — as nodes in a Peruvian *quipu*, in which the empty spaces speak. With Confucius we can see language as a wheel. The spokes centralize, but the empty spaces make the wheel.

It is thus not so much the other man's words as his silences which we have to learn in order to understand him. It is not so much our sounds which give meaning, but it is through the pauses that we will make ourselves understood. The learning of a language is more the learning of its silences than of its sounds. Only the Christian believes in the Word as coeternal Silence. Among men in time, rhythm is a law through which our conversation becomes a *yang-yin* of silence and sound.

To learn a language in a human and mature way, therefore, is to accept the responsibility for its silences and for its sounds. The gift a people gives us in teaching us their language is more a gift of the rhythm, the mode and the subtleties of its system of silences than of its system of sounds. It is an intimate gift for which we are accountable to the people who have entrusted us with their tongue. A language of which I know only the words and not the pauses is a continuous offence. It is as the caricature of a photographic negative.

It takes more time and effort and delicacy to learn the silence of a people than to learn its sounds. Some people have a special gift for this. Perhaps this explains why some missionaries, notwithstanding their efforts, never come to speak properly, to communicate delicately through silences. Although they 'speak with the accent of natives' they remain forever thousands of miles away. The learning of the grammar of silence is an art much more difficult to learn than the grammar of sounds.

As words must be learned by listening and by painful attempts at imitation of a native speaker, so silences must be acquired through a delicate openness to them. Silence has its pauses and hesitations, its rhythms and expressions and inflections; its durations and pitches, and times to be and not to be. Just as with our words, there is an analogy between our silence with men and with God. To learn the full meaning of one, we must practice and deepen the other.

First among the classification of silences is the silence of the pure listener, of womanly passivity; the silence through which the message of the other becomes 'he in us', the silence of deep interest. It is threatened by another silence – the silence of indifference, the silence of disinterest which assumes that there is nothing I want or can receive through the communication of the other. This is the ominous silence of the wife who woodenly listens to her husband relating the little things he so earnestly wants to tell her. It is the silence of the Christian who reads the gospel with the attitude that he knows it backwards and forwards. It is the silence of the stone-dead because it is unrelated to life. It is the silence of the missionary who never understood the miracle of a foreigner whose listening is a greater testimony of love than that of another who speaks. The man who shows us that he knows the rhythm of our silence is much closer to us than one who thinks that he knows how to speak.

The greater the distance between the two worlds, the more this silence of interest is a sign of love. It is easy for most Americans to listen to chit-chat about football; but it is a sign of love for a Mid-westerner to listen to the jai alai reports. The silence of the city priest on a bus listening to the report of the sickness of a goat is a gift, truly the fruit of a missionary form of long training in patience.

There is no greater distance than that between a man in prayer and God. Only when this distance dawns on consciousness can the grateful silence of patient readiness develop. This must have been the silence of the Virgin before the *Ave* which enabled her to become the eternal model of openness to the Word. Through her deep silence the Word could take Flesh.

In the prayer of silent listening, and nowhere else, can the Christian acquire the habit of this first silence from which the Word can be born in a foreign culture. This Word conceived in silence is grown in silence too.

A second great class in the grammar of silence is the silence of the Virgin after she conceived the Word – the silence from which not so much the *Fiat* as the *Magnificat* was born. It is the silence which nourishes the Word conceived rather than opening man to conception. It is the silence which closes man in on himself to allow him to prepare the Word for others. It is the silence of syntony; the silence in which we await the proper moment for the Word to be born into the world.

This silence too is threatened, not only by hurry and by desecration of multiplicity of action, but by the habit of verbal confection and mass production which has no time for it. It is threatened by the silence of cheapness which means that one word is as good as another and that words need no nursing.

The missionary, or foreigner, who uses words as they are in the dictionary does not know this silence. He is the man who looks up English words in himself when he wants to find a Spanish equivalent, rather than seeking the word which would syntonize; rather than finding the word or gesture or silence which would be understood, even if it has no equivalent in his own language or culture or background; the man who does not give the seed of a new language time to grow on the foreign soil of his soul. This is a silence *before* words, or *between* them; the silence within which words live or die. It is the silence of the slow prayer of hesitation; of prayer in which words have the courage to swim in a sea of silence. It is diametrically opposed to other forms of silence before words – the silence of the artificial flower which serves as a remembrance of words which do not grow, the pause in between repetition. It is the silence of the missionary who waits for the dispensation of the next memorized platitude because he has not made the effort to penetrate into the living language of others. The silence before words is also opposed to the silence of brewing aggression which can hardly be called silence – this too an interval used for the preparation of words, but words which divide rather than bring together. This is the silence to which the missionary is tempted who clings to the idea that in Spanish nothing means what he wants to say. It is the silence in which one verbal aggression – even though veiled – prepares the other.

The next great class in the grammar of silence we will call the silence *beyond* words. The farther we go, the farther apart does good and bad silence grow in each classification. We now have reached the silence which does not prepare any further talk. It is the silence which has said everything because there is nothing more to say. This is the silence beyond a final *yes* or a final *no*. This is the silence of love beyond words, as well as the silence of *no*, forever; the silence of heaven or of hell. It is the definite attitude of a man who faces the Word which is Silence, or the silence of a man who has obstinately turned away from Him.

Hell is this silence, deadly silence. Death in this silence is neither the deadness of a stone, indifferent to life, nor the deadness of a pressed flower, memory of life. It is the death after life, a final refusal to live. There can be noise and agitation and many words in this silence. It has only one meaning which is common to the noises it makes and the gaps between them. *No*.

There is a way in which this silence of hell threatens missionary existence. In fact with the unusual possibilities of witnessing through silence, unusual ability to destroy through it are open to the man charged with the Word in a world not his own. Missionary silence risks more: it risks becoming a hell on earth.

Ultimately, missionary silence is a gift, a gift of prayer – learned in prayer by one infinitely distant, infinitely foreign and experienced in love for men, much more distant and foreign ever than men at home. The missionary can come to forget that his silence is a gift, a gift in its deepest sense gratuitously given, a gift concretely transmitted to us by those who are willing to teach us their language. If the missionary forgets this and attempts to conquer by his own power that which only others can bestow, then his existence begins to be threatened. The man who tries to buy the language like a suit, the man who tries to conquer the language through grammar so as to speak it 'better than the natives around here', the man who forgets the analogy of the silence of God and the silence of others and does not seek its growth in prayer, is a man who tries basically to rape the culture into which he is sent, and he must expect the corresponding reactions. If he is human at all he will realize that he is in a spiritual prison, but he will not admit that he has built it around himself; rather he will accuse others of being his jailers. The wall between himself and those to whom he was sent will become ever more impenetrable. As long as he sees himself as 'missionary' he will know that he is frustrated; that he was sent but got no-where; that he is away from home but has never landed any-where; that he left his home and never reached another.

He continues to preach and is ever more aware that he is not understood, because he says what he thinks and speaks in a foreign farce of his own language. He continues to 'do things for people' and considers them ungrateful because they under-stand that he does these things to bolster his ego. His words be-come a mockery of language, an expression of the silence of death.

It requires much courage at this point to return to the patient silence of interest or to the delicacy of the silence within which words grow. Out of numbness, muteness has grown. Often out of the fear of facing the difficulty late in life of trying again to learn a language, a habit of despair is born. The silence of hell – a typically missionary version of it has been born in his heart.

At the pole opposed to despair there is the silence of love, the holding of hands of the lovers. The prayer in which the vague-ness before words has given place to the pure emptiness after them. The form of communication which opens the simple depth of the soul. It comes in flashes and it can become a lifetime – in prayer just as much as with people. Perhaps it is the only truly universal aspect of language, the only means of communication which was not touched by the curse of Babel. Perhaps it is the one way of being together with others and with the Word in which we have no more foreign accent.

There is still another silence beyond words, but the silence of the Pietà. It is not a silence of death but the silence of the mystery of death. It is not the silence of active acceptance of the will of God out of which the *Fiat* is born nor the silence of manly acceptance of Gethsemane in which obedience has its roots. The silence you as missionaries seek to acquire in this Spanish course is the silence beyond bewilderment and questions; it is a silence beyond the possibility of an answer, or even reference to a word which preceded. It is the mysterious silence through which the Lord could descend into the silence of hell, the ac-ceptance without frustration of a life, useless and wasted on Judas, a silence of freely willed powerlessness through which the world was saved. Born to redeem the world, Mary's Son had died at the hands of His people, abandoned by His friends and betrayed by Judas whom He loved but could not save – silent contemplation of the culminating paradox of the Incarnation which was useless for the redemption of at least one personal friend. The opening of the soul to this ultimate silence of the Pietà is the culmination of the slow maturing of the three previous forms of missionary silence.

5 The Seamy Side of Charity

In 1960 Pope John XXIII enjoined all United States and
Canadian religious superiors to send, within ten years, 10 per
cent of their effective strength in priests and nuns to Latin
America. This papal request was interpreted by most United
States Catholics as a call to help modernize the Latin
American Church along the lines of the North American
model. The continent on which half of all Catholics live had
to be saved from 'Castro-Communism'.

I was opposed to the execution of this order: I was
convinced that it would do serious damage to those sent, to
their clients and to their sponsors back home. I had learned
in Puerto Rico that there are only a few people who are not
stunted, or wholly destroyed, by lifelong work 'for the poor'
in a foreign country. The transfer of United States living
standards and expectations could only impede the
revolutionary changes needed, and the use of the gospel in
the service of capitalism or any other ideology was wrong.
Finally, I knew that while the United States needed much
information about all aspects of Latin America, 'missionaries'
would only hamper its collection: the feedback from
missionaries is notoriously bizarre. The projected crusade had
to be stopped.

With two friends, Miss Feodora Stancioff and Brother
Gerry Morris, I set up a centre in Cuernavaca. (We chose
this spot because of its climate, location and logistics.) Upon
the opening of our centre. I stated two of the purposes of our
undertaking. The first was to help diminish the damage
threatened by the papal order. Through our educational
programme for missionaries we intended to challenge them
to face reality and themselves, and either refuse their
assignments or – if they accepted – to be a little bit less

unprepared. Secondly, we wanted to gather sufficient influence among the decision-making bodies of mission-sponsoring agencies to dissuade them from implementing the plan.

Throughout the 1960s our experience and reputation in the intensive training of foreign professionals for assignment to South America, and the fact that we continued to be the only centre specializing in this type of education, ensured a continuing flow of students through our centre – notwithstanding our stated, basically subversive purposes.

By 1966, instead of the 10 per cent called for in 1960, barely 0·7 per cent of United States and Canadian clergy had moved south. Among the educated groups within the United States Church serious doubts had arisen about the desirability of the entire enterprise. But among bishops and the great majority of uneducated Catholics the lachrymose feedback from Latin America and an intense public relations campaign conducted from Washington continued to raise enthusiasm for the 'Help Save Latin America' cause. Under these circumstances public and intensive controversy had to be sponsored, and for that purpose I wrote the following article for the Jesuit magazine *America* in January 1967. It was deliberate timing: I knew that at the end of that month three thousand churchmen – Catholic and Protestant, from the United States and Latin America – would meet in Boston to give new impetus to their programmes, and that *Ramparts* was about to publish its exposé on Central Intelligence Agency help to student movements, especially in Latin America.

Five years ago, United States Catholics undertook a peculiar alliance for the progress of the Latin-American church. By 1970, 10 per cent of more than 225,000 priests, brothers and sisters would volunteer to be shipped south of the border. In those five years the combined United States male and female 'clergy' in South America has increased by only 1622. Halfway is a good time to determine whether a programme launched is still sailing on course, and more importantly, if its destination still seems worth while. Numerically, the programme was certainly a flop. Should this fact be a source of disappointment or relief?

The project relied on an impulse supported by uncritical imagination and sentimental judgement. A pointed finger and a 'call for 20,000' convinced many that 'Latin America needs You'. Nobody dared state clearly why, though the first published progpaganda included several references to the 'Red danger' in four pages of text. The Latin America Bureau of the National Catholic Welfare Conference attached the word 'papal' to the programme, the volunteers and the call itself.

A campaign for more funds is now being proposed. This is the moment, therefore, at which the call for 20,000 persons and the need for millions of dollars should be re-examined. Both appeals must be submitted to a public debate among United States Catholics, from bishop to widow, since they are the ones asked to supply the personnel and pay the bill. Critical thinking must prevail. Fancy and colourful campaign slogans for another collection, with their appeal to emotion, will only cloud the real issues. Let us coldly examine the American Church's outburst of charitable frenzy which resulted in the creation of 'papal' volunteers, student 'mission crusades', the annual Catholic Inter American Cooperation Programme mass assemblies, numerous diocesan missions and new religious communities.

I will not focus on details. The above programmes themselves continually study and revise minutiae. Rather I dare to point out some fundamental facts and implications of the so-called papal plan – part of the many-faceted effort to keep Latin America within the ideologies of the West. Church policy makers in the United States must face up to the socio-political consequences involved in their well-intentioned missionary ventures. They must review their vocation as Christian theologians and their actions as Western politicians.

Men and money sent with missionary motivation carry a foreign Christian image, a foreign pastoral approach and a foreign political message. They also bear the mark of North American capitalism of the 1950s. Why not, for once, consider the seamy side of charity; weigh the inevitable burdens foreign help imposes on the South American Church; taste the bitterness of the damage done by our sacrifices? If, for example, United States Catholics would simply turn from the dream of '10 per cent', and do some honest thinking about the implication of their help, the awakened awareness of intrinsic fallacies could lead to sober, meaningful generosity.

But let me be more precise. The unquestionable joys of giving and the fruits of receiving should be treated as two distinctly separate chapters. I propose to delineate only the negative results that foreign money, men and ideas produce in the South American Church, in order that the future United States programme may be tailored accordingly.

During the past five years, the cost of operating the Church in Latin America has multiplied many times. There is no precedent for a similar rate of increase in Church expenses on a continental scale. Today one Catholic university, mission society or radio chain may cost more to operate than the whole country's Church a decade ago. Most of the funds for this kind of growth came from outside and flowed from two types of sources. The first is the Church itself, which raised its income in three ways:

1. Dollar by dollar, appealing to the generosity of the faithful, as was done in Germany and the Low Countries by Adveniat, Misereor and Oostpriesterhulp. These contributions reach more than twenty-five million dollars a year.

2. Through lump sum contributions, made by individual churchmen – such as Cardinal Cushing, the outstanding example; or by institutions – such as the National Catholic Welfare Conference, transferring one million dollars from the home missions to the Latin America Bureau.

3. By assigning priests, religious and laymen, all trained at considerable cost and often backed financially in their apostolic undertakings.

This kind of foreign generosity has enticed the Latin American Church into becoming a satellite to North Atlantic cultural phenomena and policy. Increased apostolic resources intensified the need for this continued flow and created islands of apostolic well-being, each day further beyond the capacity of local support. The Latin American Church flowers anew by returning to what the Conquest stamped her: a colonial plant that blooms because of foreign cultivation. Instead of learning how to get along with less money or else close up shop, bishops are being trapped into needing more money now and bequeathing an institution impossible to run in the future. Education, the one type of investment that could give long-range returns, is conceived mostly as training for bureaucrats who will maintain the existing apparatus.

Recently I saw an example of this in a large group of Latin American priests who had been sent to Europe for advanced degrees. In order to relate the Church to the world, nine-tenths of these men were studying teaching methods – catechetics, pastoral theology or canon law – and thereby not directly advancing their knowledge of either the Church or the world. Only a few studied the Church in its history and sources, or the world as it is.

It is easy to come by big sums to build a new church in a jungle or a high school in a suburb, and then to staff the plants with new missionaries. A patently irrelevant pastoral system is artificially and expensively sustained, while basic research for a new and vital one is considered an extravagant luxury. Scholarships for non-ecclesiastical humanist studies, seed money for imaginative pastoral experimentation, grants for documentation and research to make specific constructive criticism all run the frightening risk of threatening our temporal structures, clerical plants and 'good business' methods.

Even more surprising than churchly generosity for churchly concern is a second source of money. A decade ago the Church was like an impoverished *grande dame* trying to keep up an imperial tradition of almsgiving from her reduced income. In the more than a century since Spain lost Latin America, the Church has steadily lost government grants, patrons' gifts and, finally, the revenue from its former lands. According to the colonial concept of charity, the Church lost its power to help the poor. It came to be considered a historical relic, inevitably the ally of conservative politicians.

By 1966 almost the contrary seems true – at least, at first sight. The Church has become an agent trusted to run programmes aimed at social change. It is committed enough to produce some results. But when it is threatened by real change, it withdraws rather than permit social awareness to spead like wildfire. The smothering of the Brazilian radio schools by a high Church authority is a good example.

Thus Church discipline assures the donor that his money does twice the job in the hands of a priest. It will not evaporate, nor will it be accepted for what it is: publicity for private enterprise and indoctrination to a way of life that the rich have chosen as suitable for the poor. The receiver inevitably gets the message: the 'padre' stands on the side of W. R. Grace and Company, Esso, the Alliance for Progress, democratic government, the AFL–CIO and whatever is holy in the Western pantheon.

Opinion is divided, of course, on whether the Church went heavily into social projects because it could thus obtain funds 'for the poor', or whether it went after the funds because it could thus contain Castroism and assure its institutional respectability. By becoming an 'official' agency of one kind of progress, the Church ceases to speak for the underdog who is outside all agencies but who is an ever growing majority. By accepting the power to help, the Church necessarily must denounce a Camilo Torres, who symbolizes the power of renunciation. Money thus builds the Church a 'pastoral' structure beyond its means and makes it a political power.

Superficial emotional involvement obscures rational thinking about American international 'assistance'. Healthy guilt feelings are repressed by a strangely motivated desire to 'help' in Vietnam. Finally, our generation begins to cut through the rhetoric of patriotic 'loyalty'. We stumblingly recognize the perversity of our power politics and the destructive direction of our warped efforts to impose unilaterally 'our way of life' on all. We have not yet begun to face the seamy side of clerical manpower involvement and the Church's complicity in stifling universal awakening too revolutionary to lie quietly within the 'Great Society'.

I know that there is no foreign priest or nun so shoddy in his work that through his stay in Latin America he has not enriched some life; and that there is no missionary so incompetent that through him Latin America has not made some small contribution to Europe and North America. But neither our admiration for conspicuous generosity, nor our fear of making bitter enemies out of lukewarm friends, must stop us from facing the facts. Missionaries sent to Latin America can make (1) an alien Church more foreign, (2) an overstaffed Church priest-ridden, and (3) bishops into abject beggars. Recent public discord has shattered the unanimity of the national consensus on Vietnam. I hope that public awareness of the repressive and corruptive elements contained in 'official' ecclesiastical assitance programmes will give rise to a real sense of guilt: guilt for having wasted the lives of young men and women dedicated to the task of evangelization in Latin America.

Massive, indiscriminate importation of clergy helps the ecclesiastical bureaucracy survive in its own colony, which every day becomes more foreign and comfortable. This immigration helps to transform the old-style hacienda of God (on which the people were only squatters) into the Lord's supermarket, with catechisms, liturgy and other means of grace heavily in stock. It makes contented consumers out of vegetating peasants, demanding clients out of former devotees. It lines the sacred pockets, providing refuge for men who are frightened by secular responsibility.

Churchgoers, accustomed to priests, novenas, books and culture from Spain (quite possibly to Franco's picture in the rectory), now meet a new type of executive, administrative and financial talent promoting a certain type of democracy as the Christian ideal. The people soon see that the Church is distant, alienated from them – an imported, specialized operation, financed from abroad, which speaks with a holy, because foreign, accent.

This foreign transfusion – and the hope for more – gave ecclesiastical pusillanimity a new lease of life, another chance to make the archaic and colonial system work. If North America and Europe send enough priests to fill the vacant parishes, there is no need to consider laymen – unpaid for part-time work – to

fulfil most evangelical tasks; no need to re-examine the structure
of the parish, the function of the priest, the Sunday obligation
and clerical sermon; no need to explore the use of the married
diaconate, new forms of celebration of the Word and Eucharist,
and intimate familial celebrations of conversion to the gospel in
the milieu of the home. The promise of more clergy is like a
bewitching siren. It makes the chronic surplus of clergy in Latin
America invisible and it makes it impossible to diagnose this
surplus as the gravest illness of the Church. Today, this pessi-
mistic evaluation is slightly altered by a courageous and imaginative few – non-Latins among them – who see, study and strive
for true reform.

A large proportion of Latin American Church personnel are
presently employed in private institutions that serve the middle
and upper classes and frequently produce highly respectable
profits; this on a continent where there is a desperate need for
teachers, nurses and social workers in public institutions that
serve the poor. A large part of the clergy are engaged in bureaucratic functions, usually related to peddling sacraments, sacra-
mentals and superstitious 'blessings'. Most of them live in
squalor. The Church, unable to use its personnel in pastorally
meaningful tasks, cannot even support its priests and the 670
bishops who govern them. Theology is used to justify this system,
canon law to administer it and foreign clergy to create a world-
wide consensus on the necessity of its continuation.

A healthy sense of values empties the seminaries and the ranks
of the clergy much more effectively than does a lack of discipline
and generosity. In fact, the new mood of well-being makes the
ecclesiastical career more attractive to the self-seeker. Bishops
turn servile beggars, become tempted to organize safaris, and
hunt out foreign priests and funds for constructing such anomalies as minor seminaries. As long as such expeditions succeed, it
will be difficult if not impossible, to take the emotionally harder
road: to ask ourselves honestly if we need such a game.

Exporting Church employees to Latin America masks a universal and unconscious fear of a new Church. North and South
American authorities, differently motivated but equally fearful,
become accomplices in maintaining a clerical and irrelevant
Church. Sacralizing employees and property, this Church be-

comes progressively more blind to the possibilities of sacralizing person and community.

It is hard to help by refusing to give alms. I remember once having stopped food distribution from sacristies in an area where there was great hunger. I still feel the sting of an accusing voice saying: 'Sleep well for the rest of your life with the death of dozens of children on your conscience.' Even some doctors prefer aspirins to radical surgery. They feel no guilt having the patient die of cancer, but fear the risk of applying the knife. The courage needed today is that expressed by Daniel Berrigan, S.J., writing of Latin America: 'I suggest we stop sending anyone or anything for three years and dig in and face our mistakes and find out how not to canonize them.'

From six years' experience in training hundreds of foreign missionaries assigned to Latin America, I know that real volunteers increasingly want to face the truth that puts their faith to the test. Superiors who shift personnel by their administrative decisions but do not have to live with the ensuing deceptions are emotionally handicapped facing these realities.

The United States Church must face the painful side of generosity: the burden that a life gratuitously offered imposes on the recipient. The men who go to Latin America must humbly accept the possibility that they are useless or even harmful, although they give all they have. They must accept the fact that a limping ecclesiastical assistance programme uses them as palliatives to ease the pain of a cancerous structure, the only hope being that the prescription will give the organism enough time and rest to initiate a spontaneous healing. It is far more probable that the pharmacist's pill will both stop the patient from seeking a surgeon's advice and addict him to the drug.

Foreign missionaries increasingly realize that they heeded a call to plug the holes in a sinking ship because the officers did not dare launch the life rafts. Unless this is clearly seen, men who obediently offer the best years of their lives will find themselves tricked into a useless struggle to keep a doomed liner afloat as it limps through uncharted seas.

We must acknowledge that missionaries can be pawns in a world ideological struggle and that it is blasphemous to use the gospel to prop up any social or political system. When men and money are sent into a society within the framework of a programme, they bring ideas that live after them. It has been pointed out, in the case of the Peace Corps, that the cultural mutation catalysed by a small foreign group might be more effective than all the immediate services it renders. The same can be true of the North American missionary—close to home, having great means at his disposal, frequently on a short-term assignment – who moves into an area of intense United States cultural and economic colonization. He is part of this sphere of influence and, at times, intrigue. Through the United States missionary, the United States shadows and colours the public image of the Church. The influx of United States missionaries coincides with the Alliance for Progress, Camelot and CIA projects and looks like a baptism of all three. The Alliance appears directed by Christian justice and is not seen for what it is: a deception designed to maintain the *status quo*, albeit variously motivated. During the programme's first five years, the net capital leaving Latin America has tripled. The programme is too small to permit even the achievement of a threshold of sustained growth. It is a bone thrown to the dog, that he remain quiet in the back-yard of the Americas.

Within these realities, the United States missionary tends to fulfil the traditional role of a colonial power's lackey chaplain. The dangers implicit in Church use of foreign money assume the proportion of caricature when this aid is administered by a 'gringo' to keep the 'underdeveloped' quiet. It is, of course, too much to ask of most Americans that they make sound, clear and outspoken criticisms of United States socio-political aggression in Latin America, even more difficult that they do so without the bitterness of the expatriate or the opportunism of the turncoat.

Groups of United States missionaries cannot avoid projecting the image of 'United States outposts'. Only individual Americans mixed in with local men could avoid this distortion. The missionary of necessity is an 'undercover' agent—albeit unconscious – for United States social and political consensus. But, consciously and purposely, he wishes to bring the values of his Church to South America; adaptation and selection seldom reach the level of questioning the values themselves.

The situation was not so ambiguous ten years ago, when in good conscience mission societies were channels for the flow of traditional United States Church hardware to Latin America. Everything from the Roman collar to parochial schools, from United-States catechisms to Catholic universities, was considered saleable merchandise in the new Latin American market. Not much salesmanship was needed to convince the Latin bishops to give the 'Made in USA' label a try.

In the meantime however, the situation has changed considerably. The United-States Church is shaking from the first findings of a scientific and massive self-evaluation. Not only methods and institutions, but also the ideologies that they imply, are subject to examination and attack. The self-confidence of the American ecclesiastical salesman is therefore shaky. We see the strange paradox of a man attempting to implant, in a really different culture, structures and programmes that are now rejected in the country of their origin. (I recently heard of a Catholic grammar school being planned by United States personnel in a Central American city parish where there are already a dozen public schools.)

There is an opposite danger, too. Latin America can no longer tolerate being a haven for United States liberals who cannot make their point at home, an outlet for apostles too 'apostolic' to find their vocation as competent professionals within their own community. The hardware salesman threatens to dump second-rate imitations of parishes, schools and catechisms – outmoded even in the United States – all around the continent. The travelling escapist threatens further to confuse a foreign world with his superficial protests, which are not viable even at home.

The American Church of the Vietnam generation finds it difficult to engage in foreign aid without exporting either its solutions or its problems. Both are prohibitive luxuries for developing nations. Mexicans, to avoid offending the sender, pay high duties for useless or unasked-for gifts sent them by well-meaning American friends. Gift givers must think not of this moment and of this need, but in terms of a full generation of the future effects. Gift planners must ask if the global value of the gift in men, money and ideas is worth the price the recipient will ultimately have to pay for it. As Father Berrigan suggests, the rich and powerful can decide not to give; the poor can hardly refuse to accept. Since almsgiving conditions the beggar's mind, the

Latin American bishops are not entirely at fault in asking for misdirected and harmful foreign aid. A large measure of the blame lies with the underdeveloped ecclesiology of United States clerics who direct the 'sale' of American good intentions.

The United States Catholic wants to be involved in an ecclesiologically valid programme, not in subsidiary political and social programmes designed to influence the growth of developing nations according to anybody's social doctrine, be it even described as the Pope's. The heart of the discussion is therefore not *how* to send more men and money, but rather *why* they should be sent at all. The Church, in the meantime, is in no critical danger. We are tempted to shore up and salvage structures rather than question their purpose and truth. Hoping to glory in the works of our hands, we feel guilty, frustrated and angry when part of the building starts to crumble. Instead of believing in the Church, we frantically attempt to construct it according to our own cloudy cultural image. We want to build community, relying on techniques, and are blind to the latent desire for unity that is striving to express itself among men. In fear, we plan *our* Church with statistics, rather than trustingly search for the living Church which is right among us.

6 The Vanishing Clergyman

I drafted this paper in 1959 and published it, at the request of a friend, in the *Critic* of Chicago, in 1967.

Great changes must take place in the structure of the Catholic Church if it is to survive. I believe that such changes will come about and, moreover, that they can now be visualized in terms consistent with the most radically traditional theology. Nevertheless, such changes would thoroughly upset the idea of the Catholic Church deeply imbedded in the imagination of Catholics and non-Catholics alike.

One could have spoken about these changes in abstract terms. I preferred to illustrate my general thesis by indicating what, in my opinion, will happen to the 'clergyman', to his status, his role, his self-image, his professional standing. I wanted to raise a question, clearly and simply. But I had further reasons for making my statement through a concrete example.

For one, I did not want to say anything *theologically* new, daring or controversial. Only a spelling-out of the *social* consequences would make a thesis as orthodox as mine sufficiently controversial to be discussed within the overwhelming conservative majority of the Church.

A second reason for my decision to focus on the clergy was the attempt to render the discussion relevant to the 'Catholic left'. Suggestions for a reform of the Catholic priesthood abounded in these quarters in the mid-1960s. The majority of these suggestions seemed neither sufficiently revolutionary to be worth while (a married clergy, priests engaged in social action or revolution) nor sufficiently faithful to fundamental traditional positions – which I would not like to see compromised (such as the value of freely chosen celibacy, the episcopal structure of the Church, the permanence of priestly ordination).

The Roman Church is the world's largest non-governmental bureaucracy. It employs 1·8 million full-time workers – priests, brothers, sisters and laymen. These employees work within a corporate structure which an American business consultant firm rates as among the most efficiently operated organizations in the world. The institutional Church functions on a par with the General Motors Company and the Chase Manhattan Bank. Recognition of this fact is accepted, sometimes, with pride. But to some, the machine-like smoothness itself seems to discredit the Church. Men suspect that it has lost its relevance to the gospel and to the world. Wavering, doubt and confusion reign among its directors, functionaries and employees. The giant begins to totter before it collapses.

Some church personnel react to the breakdown with pain, anguish and fright. Some make heroic efforts and tragic sacrifices to prevent it. Some, regretfully or joyfully, interpret the phenomenon as a sign of the disappearance of the Roman Church itself. I would like to suggest that we welcome the disappearance of institutional bureaucracy in a spirit of deep joy. In this essay, I shall describe some aspects of what is taking place in the Church, and suggest ways in which the Church could seek a radical reorganization in some of its structures. I am not recommending essential changes in the Church; even less do I suggest its dissolution. The complete disappearance of its visible structure would contradict sociological law and divine mandate. But change does entail much more than drastic amendment or updating reform if the Church is to respond to God's call and contemporary man. I shall outline certain possible changes, solidly rooted in the origins of the Church, and boldly reaching out to the necessities of tomorrow's society. Acceptance of this kind of reform will require the Church to live the evangelical poverty of Christ. At the same time, the Church, sensitive to the process of the world's progressive socialization, will come to have a deep respect for, and joyful acceptance of, this phenomenon.

The institutional Church is in trouble. The very persons on whose loyalty and obedience the efficiency structure depends increasingly abandon it. Until the early 1960s, the 'defections' were relatively rare. Now they are common. Tomorrow they may be the pattern. After a personal drama played out in the intimacy of conscience, more and more ecclesiastical employees will decide to sacrifice the emotional, spiritual and financial security which the system benevolently provided for them. I suspect that within this generation these persons will have become a majority of the Church's personnel.

The problem lies not with the 'spirit' of the world, nor with any failure in generosity among the 'defectors', but rather with the *structure itself*. This can be taken as an almost aprioristic conclusion, since the present structures developed as a response to past situations vastly different from our own. Further, our world continually accelerates its rapid changes of societal structures, in the context of which the Church must carry out its real functions. To see the situation more clearly, I shall focus my attention on the nature and function of ministry, the complex channel through which the Church touches the world. We can thus gain some insight into the Church of tomorrow.

It seems evident that basic and accepted concepts of ministry in the Church are clearly inadequate. Quantitatively, for example, the Church really does not need the present number of full-time employees who work in its operational structure. More fundamentally, the situation suggests the need for a deep reappraisal of the elements which make up the current idea of the priest as the Church's basic representative in the world – a concept still maintained in the conciliar decrees. Specifically there is need for a re-examination of the relation between sacramental ministry and full-time personnel, between ministry and celibacy, and between ministry and theological education.

Today it is assumed that most if not all of the Church's ministerial operations must be carried out by full-time underpaid employees who possess a kind of theological education and who accept an ecclesiastical law of celibacy. In order to begin a search for new directions which are more evangelically and sociologically relevant, I shall discuss separately four aspects of the problem: the radical reduction in the number of persons dependent on the Church for their livelihood; the ordination to sacramental ministry of men independently employed in the world; the special and unique renunciation implied in perpetual celibacy; the relation between sacramental ministry and theological education.

The clergy: desire for more and need for less

The Church's personnel enjoy remarkable privileges. Every teenager who seeks employment among the clergy is almost automatically guaranteed a status which confers a variety of personal and social benefits, most of which come with advancing age, not because of competence or productivity. His rights to social and economic security are more far-reaching than plans for the guaranteed income.

Ecclesiastical employees live in comfortable Church-owned housing, are assured preferential treatment in Church-owned and operated health services, are mostly trained in ecclesiastical educational institutions, and are buried in hallowed ground – after which they are prayed for. The habit or collar, not competent productivity, assures one's status and living. An employment market, more diversified than any existing corporation, caters to the employee, discriminating against laymen who do not share his ritual initiation. Laymen who work in the ecclesiastical structure are recognized as possessing some few 'civil rights', but their careers depend principally on their ability to play the role of Uncle Toms.

Recently the Roman Church has followed the example of some Protestant churches in shifting more of its employees from parish work to paper pushing. At the same time, the traditional demand for increased personnel at the parish level and the simultaneously burgeoning process of overinflated bureaucratic machinery masks the increasing irrelevance of both these aspects of the structure. Organizational explosion results in a feverish search for more personnel and money. We are urged to beg God to send more employees into the bureaucratic system and to inspire the faithful to pay the cost. Personally, I cannot ask God for these 'benefits'. The inherently self-perpetuating expansion of Church personnel operates well enough without additional help, and only serves to make an already overstaffed Church more priest-ridden, thereby debilitating the Church's mission in today's world.

The Vatican itself best illustrates the complex problem. Post-conciliar administrative growth supersedes and supplants the old machinery. Since the end of the Council, the twelve venerable curial congregations have been increased by the addition of numerous intermeshing and overlapping post-conciliar organs – commissions, councils, consultative bodies, committees, assemblies, synods. This bureaucratic maze becomes ungovernable. Good. Perhaps this will help us to see that principles of corporate government are not applicable to the Body of Christ. It is even less appropriate to see His Vicar as the chief executive of a corporation than as a Byzantine king. Clerical technocracy is even further from the gospel than priestly aristocracy. And we may come to recognize that efficiency corrupts Christian testimony more subtly than power.

At a time when even the Pentagon seeks to reduce its manpower pool by contracting specific jobs in the open market of industry and research, the Vatican launches a drive towards greater self-contained institutional diversification and proliferation. The central administration of this top-heavy organizational giant passes out of the hands of the 'venerable congregations' staffed by Italian career priests into those of clerical specialists recruited from all over the world. The Pontifical Curia of the Middle Ages becomes a contemporary corporation's planning and administrative headquarters.

One of the paradoxical aspects of today's structure is that the organization priest is also a member of the aristocracy of the only feudal power left in the Western world – a power whose sovereign status was recognized in the Lateran conventions. Further, this same power increasingly uses a diplomatic structure – one originally developed to represent the Church's interests *vis-à-vis* other sovereign states – in order to offer services to the emerging international agencies, such as the Food and Agriculture Organization, UNICEF, UNESCO and to the United Nations itself. This development demands more and more employees for a wider range of jobs, requiring even more specialized education for the recruits. The hierarchy, accustomed to absolute control over its employees, seeks to staff these positions with captive clergy. But the big push on more intensive recruitment runs head-on into a strong and contrary trend: yearly almost as many trained personnel leave as are recruited. Hence we see the reluctant acceptance of submissive and obedient laymen to fill the gap.

Some individuals explain clerical 'defections' as the elimina-

tion of undesirable elements. Others blame the various contemporary mystiques of the world. The institution instinctively
attempts to explain this loss and the concomitant vocation 'crisis'
in terms flattering to itself. Then too one needs strong justification for the enthusiastic and emotional drives for more 'vocations'. Few wish to admit that the collapse of an overextended
and disproportionate clerical framework is a clear sign of its
irrelevance. Fewer see that the Pope himself would grow in
evangelical stature and fidelity in proportion as his power to
affect social issues in the world and his administrative command
in the Church decline.

Changes on the institutional periphery are as faithful to
'Parkinson's Law' as changes in Rome: work grows with available personnel. Since the end of the Council, attempts at collegial
decentralization have resulted in a wildly uncontrolled growth
of bureaucracy reaching to the local level. Latin America offers
a grotesque example. A generation ago Latin American bishops
travelled to Rome about every ten years to report to the Pope.
Their only other contacts with Rome were the stylized petitions
for indulgences of dispensations, channelled through the Nuncio,
and occasional Curial Visitators. Today a complex Roman Com-
mission for Latin America coordinates subcommissions of European and American bishops in the power balance with the Latin
American Bishops' Assembly. This is organized in a board
(*Consejo Episcopal Latinoamericano*) and numerous commissions, secretariats, institutes and delegations. CELAM itself is
the crown of sixteen national bishops' conferences, some of
which are even more complex in bureaucratic organization. The
entire structure is designed to facilitate occasional consultations
among bishops, in order that, returning to their dioceses, they
might act with greater independence and originality. The real
results are rather different. The bishops develop the bureaucratic
mentality necessary to keep up with the merry-go-round character of the increasingly frequent meetings. The newly created
organisms absorb large numbers of trained grass-roots personnel
into clerical staff and planning services. Restrictive and unimag-
inative central control replaces creative and fresh approaches in
the local churches.

In the entire Church a clergy survives partly because priestly service at the altar is united with clerical power and privilege. This union helps to maintain the existing structure. Church-employed priests assure a personnel supply to fill places in the corporate structure. Priest–clerics assure the continuance and abundance of career-minded churchmen. The ordination of self-supporting laymen to sacramental functions would eventually destroy the bureaucracy. But men whose mentality and security have been formed and maintained by the system instinctively fear the ordination of persons who remain in secular employment. The diocesan chancellor, the Catholic Charities director and the pastor feel as much threatened by declericalization as the Catholic university president, the supplier of ecclesiastical finery and furnishings, and such civic leaders as Saul Alinsky. In different ways all are supported by, or depend upon, the power and prestige of the clergy. Nevertheless, the ordination of secularly employed men may be one of the Church's great advances.

Today, some clerics begin to see that they are smothered in a scandalous and unnecessary security combined with restrictive and unacceptable controls. A priest, well-trained in theology, is assured life-long support, but it may be as an accountant, and not as a theologian, if he has been caught reading certain 'suspect' foreign authors. Conversely, a Latin American bishop may send a priest for sociological studies in Europe and then decide to create a diocesan department of research to use the new talent he has acquired.

Some priests are dissatisfied with their work, either because their freedom to do a good job is curtailed, or because they feel unprepared for the specific task assigned them. In the first instance, better job descriptions are proposed as a remedy; in the second, better education for the jobholder. Both solutions are no more than misguided palliatives. The question must be asked: should not this job be dropped from Church control, and the cleric either fired or challenged to compete for it – under secular control and conditions? Of course if we continue to present system, we are still stuck with our problem: the dissatisfied cleric.

Therefore the next five years will see a proliferation of re-training programmes for the clergy. The outmoded product of novitiate and seminary needs different skills and attitudes to fit into the 'new' Church: a multiplying growth of specialized commissions, bureaux and secretariats. But it's going to be a problem, selling the programmes. The men themselves are beginning to say: perhaps I need training to move into the *secular* world, to support myself as other men in society, to act as an adult in the world.

Dioceses and religious congregations increasingly use business consultants, whose criteria of success are taken from the American Management Association, and whose premise is that the present structure must be maintained. The resulting clergy in-service training is essentially repressive, ideologically biased and directed toward efficient Church growth. Present ecclesiastical training improves a man's ability to operate a more complex machine. A retreat only serves to confirm a man's *personal* commitment to the structure. An *adult* formation concept is needed, one which would lead men to search for the right questions. Is this structure rooted in routine or revelations? Should I, a man totally at the service of the Church, stay in the structure in order to subvert it, or leave in order to *live* the model of the future? The Church needs men seeking this kind of conscious and critical awareness – men deeply faithful to the Church, living a life of insecurity and risk, free from hierarchical control, working for the eventual 'disestablishment' of the Church from within. The very few such groups in existence today are branded as disloyal and dangerous by the clerical mentality.

A good example of such subsersive education is provided by the Sister Formation Movement in the United States. This movement acts as a major factor working towards the secularization of the American Church from within. In the mid-1950s, a group of sisters set up a lobby to pressure for advanced professional education of religious. When this had been achieved, and the brothers and sisters returned to their communities with Ph.D.s, they were competent to apply for academic jobs anywhere. They no longer had to rely on preferential treatment traditionally accorded in Church institutions to religious, irrespective of their talent or professional training.

Many of these trained persons become conscious of ridiculous restrictions imposed upon them and their institutions by the clerical mind and ecclesiastical control. Some saw themselves facing the necessity of leaving their communities in order to live a meaningful and relevant career. Others chose to work for the liberation of their institutions from repressive and destructive Church control. The former were branded as defectors and the latter as subversives. Finally, religious congregations began to allow their members to seek temporary or permanent employment of their own choice in the open market, while remaining members of the community. This will lead to the persons themselves choosing their companions, places of residence, and form of community living.

Many superiors of religious women have recently begun to understand the signs of the times. Suddenly they see the possibility that the era of religious congregations might be over. Bishops are not yet aware that an analogous movement is at work among the clergy. But this movement is weaker and less sophisticated, because of the retarded nature of the American clergy. For several generations they have been pampered into unquestioning submission by their middle-class comfort and security.

Today some priests believe that they might be better ministers if they worked at secular jobs that entail real social and economic responsibility. A priest–artist, for example, questions the bishop's right to employ him as a scribe, or to suspend him if he seeks real work in Greenwich Village. These trends produce a double effect among the clergy. The committed man is moved to renounce his clerical privileges, thereby risking suspension, and the mediocre man is moved to clamour for more fringe benefits and less adult responsibility, thereby settling down more comfortably in his clerical security.

Seeing the evangelical and social contradictions in the bureaucracy, some courageously face the possible alternatives. I know many who desire full-time jobs in poverty programmes, as community organizers, teachers, researchers, professional men. They desire to earn their livings and live as celibate laymen, while exercising their ministerial functions on a part-time basis in the service of the faithful, and under the bishop's authority. They ask if the system is sensitive enough to the real society to evolve a new form of radical and personal declericalization which would entail neither suspension from orders nor dispensation from celibacy.

what does this really mean?

Of course, such radical secularization threatens the existing parochial system. It would encourage the imaginative and generous to strike out on their own and thereby leave the clerical and outdated ecclesiastical structure in the hands of those who choose security and routine. It would frighten both bureaucratic bishops and rebellious DuBays. The bishops desire more clerics, but reject any demands for employee privileges, especially the notion of unionized power. The attitudes of both the bishops and the DuBays necessarily imply the furtherance of the clerical system.

Men in secular society sometimes recognize a real hypocrisy in this system. Groups founded for social protest and revolutionary action find the clergy suspect. The former, when they act, freely risk their careers for a cause to which their conscience impels them. The priest or nun who suddenly becomes aware that a real world exists and belatedly joins such actions risks a gentle reprimand at most. Usually the more enlightened superior is quite pleased and happy with his 'courageous' subject. It is much cheaper to permit a few naïve protesters, rather than face the frightening price of Christian institutional testimony to society.

To begin the task of giving this testimony, may we pray for an increase of priests who choose 'radical' secularization? For priests who leave the Church in order to pioneer the church of the future? For priests who, faithfully dedicated to and loving the Church, risk misunderstanding and suspension? For priests, full of hope, capable of such actions without becoming hard and embittered? For extraordinary priests, willing to live today the ordinary life of tomorrow's priest?

The shape of the future ministry

An adult layman, ordained to the ministry, will preside over the 'normal' Christian community of the future. The ministry will be an exercise of leisure rather than a job. The 'diaconia' will supplant the parish as the fundamental institutional unit in the church. The periodic meeting of friends will replace the Sunday assembly of strangers. A self-supporting dentist, factory worker, professor, rather than a church-employed scribe or functionary, will preside over the meeting. The minister will be a man mature in Christian wisdom through his lifelong participation in an intimate liturgy, rather than a seminary graduate formed professionally through 'theological' formulae. Marriage and the education of growing children, rather than the acceptance of celibacy as a legal condition for ordination, will confer responsible leadership on him.

I foresee the face-to-face meeting of families around a table, rather than the impersonal attendance of a crowd around an altar. Celebration will sanctify the dining room, rather than consecrated buildings the ceremony. This does not mean that *all* churches will be converted into theatres or real-estate white elephants. For example, the Bishop of Cuernavaca believes that Latin-American tradition requires the existence of the cathedral church as a kind of testimony in stone, whose beauty and majesty reflect the splendour of Christian truth.

Present pastoral structures have been largely determined by ten centuries of a clerical and celibate priesthood. In 1964 the Council took a suggestive step towards changing this pattern when it approved a married diaconate. The decree is ambiguous since it could lead to a proliferation of second-rate clergy without making any significant change in present structures. But it can also lead to the ordination of adult, self-supporting men. The danger would be in developing a clerical church-supported diaconate, thereby delaying the necessary and inevitable secularization of the ministry.

The 'ordinary' future priest, earning his living outside the church, will preside over a weekly meeting of a dozen deacons in his house. Together they will read the Scripture, then study and comment upon the bishop's weekly instruction. After the meeting, when it includes Mass, each deacon will take the Sacrament to his own home, where he will keep it with his crucifix and Bible. The priest will visit his various 'diaconias' and preside at their occasional Mass. At times a number of the 'diaconias' will meet for a more solemn Mass in a rented hall or in a cathedral.

Freed of present executive and administrative duties, both the bishop and his priests will have time for occasional celebrations. The bishop will be able to prepare and circulate his weekly selection from the Fathers and the outline for discussion. He and his priests will together prepare the home liturgy for the 'diaconias'. These changes will require a different attitude towards weekly Mass obligation as well as a re-evaluation of present ritual practices of penance.

Present canon law provides for the ordination of those whose lifelong livelihood has been guaranteed by the Church, and of those whose own estate is sufficient to support them. To restrict ordination to this kind of economic independence seems anomalous, if not revolting, in today's society. Today, a man supports himself by working at a job in the world, not by performing a role in a hierarchy. It is certainly not contrary to the purposes of canon law to consider professional ability or earned social security as sufficient sign of independence for ordination.

The sacramental ministry of ordained laymen will open our eyes to a completely new understanding of the traditional 'opposition' between pastor and layman in the Church. As we move beyond both these concepts, we shall clearly see their transitory character. The Council, summarizing a historical development of the last hundred years, attempted to define the clerical priest and the unordained layman in two separate documents. But the future will achieve, from the apparent antithesis, a new synthesis which transcends present categories.

The current ecclesiastical imagination is still inadquate for defining this new function – the lay priest, Sunday priest, part-time or secularized minister, ordained non-cleric. Principally he will be the minister of sacrament and word, not the jack-of-all-trades, superficially responding to a bewildering variety of social and psychological roles. With his emergence the Church will finally free itself from the restrictive system of benefices. More importantly the Church will have abandoned the complex series of services which have resulted in the minister becoming an artificial appendix to established social functions. The ordained layman will make the Catholic parson pastorally superfluous.

The Church awakens anew in the city. Traditional pastoral analogies become anomalies in the asphalt, steel and concrete context of city life. Urban renewal and new experiences of community call for another look at older terminology. Kings, crowns and staffs have lost their meaning. Men are not subjects of sovereigns, and they impatiently question how they can be sheep led by a shepherd. The Church's community-creating functions break down when supported by symbols whose driving force lies in an authority structure. Sophisticated urban Catholics do not seek authoritative guidance for community action from a pastor. They know that social action is ecumenical and secular in motive, method and goal. The Protestant minister or the secularist professional can possess better credentials of leadership.

Theologically literate persons no longer seek moral guidance from a priest. They themselves think. Frequently, they have long ago surpassed the priest in theological formation. Parents with a good liberal education are increasingly sceptical of entrusting their children to the clerical system of 'professional' catechesis. If children can be evangelized, parents see that they are called to the task, and possess the knowledge and faith to carry it out.

No thinking Catholic questions accepting the ritual which recognizes that a man has received divine power to moderate a meeting of Christians or preside over the celebration of a sacrament. But men begin to reject the claims of a pastor who, because of his ordination or consecration, feigns competency to deal with *any* problem of his heterogeneous congregation, be it the parish, the diocese or the world.

The reorganization of contemporary life frees men to accept a vocation for part-time ministerial functions. Leisure time increases with reduced working hours, early retirement and more inclusive social-security benefits – time available for the preparation and exercise of Christian ministry in a pluralistic and secular society.

It is apparent that many objections can be raised. The lay priest or deacon might wish to withdraw from the ministry, he might publicly sin, he or his wife might become divisive factors in the Christian community. Present canon law implicitly contains the solution – let him be 'suspended' from his functions. Suspension must become an option for both the man and the community, not just a punishment reserved to the bishop. The ordained minister might feel called to take a controversial position on some secular matter in society, and thereby cease to be a fitting symbol of sacramental unity. He might in conscience feel that he must become a sign of contradiction, not only *to* the world, but also *in* the world. Let him or the community freely seek suspension. The community which has recognized his charisma and presented him to the bishop, can also respect his liberty of conscience and allow him to act accordingly. He himself, as minister, has no special benefits, income, or status to defend. His daily life has not been determined by his priesthood. Rather, the latter has been characterized by his secular commitment.

Ministry and celibacy

Man finds it difficult to separate what habit or custom has united. The union of the clerical state, holy orders and celibacy in the life of the Church has confused the understanding of the individual realities involved and prevented us from seeing the possibility of their separation. The clergy have stood on their socio-economic status and power, defending their exclusive right to the priesthood. We seldom see *theological* arguments directed against the ordained laymen, except perhaps in reference to the inadequacy of the term itself. Only Catholic clerics who wish to marry, and married Protestant ministers who fear to lose their clerical status, defend the extension of ecclesiastical social security to a married minister.

The link between celibacy and priestly orders now comes under heavy attack, in spite of authoritative statements defending it. Exegetical, pastoral and social arguments are marshalled against it. By their action, increasing numbers of priests not only deny it, but also abandon both celibacy and the ministry. The problem is admittedly complex, since two realities of faith – sacramental ministry of priesthood and the personal mystery of extraordinary renunciation – meet. Our secular language breaks down in the delicate analysis of their mutual relationships. The formulation and discussion of three separate questions may help us to see the proper distinctions and lead us to understand the nature of the relationships involved. The choice of voluntary celibacy, the institution of religious communities and the legal prescription of a celibate priesthood must be seen separately.

At all times in the Church, men and women have freely renounced marriage 'for the sake of the kingdom'. Consistent with such an action, they simply 'explain' their decision as a personal realization of an intimate vocation from God. This mysterious experience of vocation must be distinguished from the discursive formulation of reasons to 'justify' such a decision. To many, such arguments appear meaningless. This conclusion leads men to abandon their commitment to celibacy. The defenders of celibacy frequently interpret this action as manifesting a poor or weak faith among contemporary Catholics. On the contrary, it may just as well be evidence of the purification of their faith. Men now see through the alleged motives – sociological, psychological and mythological – for celibacy, and recognize their irrelevance to true Christian renunciation. Renunciation of marriage is not economically necessary for service to the poor, nor legally a condition for the ordained ministry, nor significantly convenient for higher studies. Persons who acted on these motives now fail to see their value and relevance. Celibacy can no longer enlist social approval in its defence.

Psychological motives formerly invoked to justify the superiority of sexual abstinence are hardly acceptable today. Many celibates now see that they initially refused marriage because they were repelled, afraid, unprepared or simply not attracted. Now they choose marriage, either because of a more mature understanding of themselves, or to prove their original feelings wrong. They no longer see themselves as heroes to their parents, because they are 'faithful', nor as pariahs, because they 'defect'.

Comparative studies in religion reveal many 'reasons' for sexual renunciation throughout human history. These may be reduced to ascetical, magical and mystical motives. Oftentimes they are 'religious', but hardly related to the Christian faith. The ascetic renounces marriage for freedom to pray; the magician, to 'save' a Chinese baby through his sacrifice; the mystic, to seek exclusive bridal intimacy with 'the All'. Contemporary man knows that sexual renunciation does not make prayer more intimate, love more ardent or graces received more abundant.

Today the Christian who renounces marriage and children for the kingdom's sake seeks no abstract or concrete *reason* for his decision. His choice is pure risk in faith, the result of the intimate and mysterious experience of his heart. He chooses to live *now* the absolute poverty every Christian hopes to experience at the hour of death. His life does not *prove* God's transscendence; rather, his whole being expresses faith in it. His decision to renounce a spouse is as intimate and incommunicable as another's decision to prefer *his* spouse over all others.

The Church has evolved two devices to control an evangelical charisma: the social and juridical organization of religious communities, and the ritual celebration of vows. Religious orders provide a community structure within which the member is supposed to deepen his baptismal commitment to sanctity, and make himself available for the manpower pool controlled by his superior. This captive personnel force enabled the religious congregations to conduct benevolent and business enterprises. Now it appears that these institutional works will disappear even faster than parish, diocesan and curial structures, as more and more members leave to fulfil their vocations in the open job market.

Christians desiring to live evangelical celibacy see fewer reasons for joining the established, juridical communities – even secular institutes – but they do recognize the necessity to band together with others of like mind, temporarily or permanently, to seek mutual support in their common and difficult spiritual adventure. Those established religious communities which remain in existence will maintain houses of intensive prayer, available as retreat houses, spiritual training centres, monasteries or deserts. To arrive at this kind of Christian poverty and witness, the congregations legislate their impending demise by approving shortened skirts, changing prayer schedules and experimenting in social action. Perhaps this legislative sniping at superficialities will serve to diminish the pain of those in the dying structure, easing their stay to the bitter end.

As the traditionally accepted reasons for maintaining the present juridical communities evaporate, other means of making a lifelong vow will be explored. The Church has traditionally accepted the possibility of the private vow. Less and less shall we see this in exclusively legal terms. As living a vow moves from clerical structures to a life of renunciation in the secular world, it seems more appropriate to signify the joyful acceptance of this kind of commitment not through a juridical act creating legal obligations but through a liturgical celebration of a mystical fact. The Church moves in this direction as vows become less public, solemn and binding. Today any religious receives his dispensation when he states that he does not intend to keep his vow. Formerly vows were treated as public renunciations of rights; now they seem more like public statements of conditional intentions. The religious makes much ado of the fact that he is not married and that he will not marry – unless, of course, he changes his mind. We move from a religious 'state' to a religious 'stage'. The confusion and pharisaic legalism is a sorry testimony to the world.

The celebration of a vow should be a rite established by the Church, publicly testifying to belief in the authenticity of a particular Christian vocation and charisma. Only exceptional persons, after many years of *living* their renunciation in secular life, should be admitted to such a liturgical celebration. The Church thereby publicly manifests its willingness to entrust the testimony of a mystery to the fidelity of these new 'monks'. Only then shall we return to the real and close analogy between Christian marriage and renunciation. Both sacraments will celebrate the Christian's full awareness of the depth and totality of a commitment he has established and lived in the real society of men.

A large segment of the thinking Church questions the tie between celibacy and the priesthood. The Pope insists on their connection. Neither doctrine nor tradition gives definitive support to his position. I believe that the emergence of a new pastoral Church depends largely on compliance with his directive during our generation. His position helps assure the speedy death of the clergy.

To counteract the trends of declining vocations and clerical dropouts, many solutions are proposed: married clergy, sisters and laymen in pastoral tasks, brighter appeals in vocation campaigns, world-wide distribution of existing clergy. All are simply so many pusillanimous attempts to rejuvenate a dying structure.

During our generation, at least, there is no need to consider the ordination of married men to the priesthood. We have more than enough unmarried ones. Ordaining married priests would slow up any real pastoral reform. But there is a second, and more delicate, reason for this decision. Thousands of priests now reject celibacy, and present the painful spectacle of men trained for sexual abstinence groping belatedly into big-risk marriage.

The Church dispenses them secretly, arbitrarily and awkwardly. They are forbidden further exercise of their orders. Having chosen marriage, they *could* still exercise priestly functions, but they would cease to be models – except perhaps to others like themselves.

The real need here is to clarify and liberalize the process by which the Church allows a priest to marry. Further, all must see that the good of the Church requires the 'ex-priest' to abandon both clerical security and ministerial function. This is as difficult for the priest who 'wants out' without accepting the concomitant consequences, as it is for the bishop who wants to 'hang onto' his priest at all costs. The clerical mass exodus will only last as long as the present clerical system exists. During this time ordination of married men would be a sad mistake. The resulting confusion would only delay needed radical reforms.

The one institution which has no future in the Church and which is at the same time most impervious to any radical reform, today loses an increasing number of its men because of the legislation of celibacy. The overall seriousness of the seminary crisis, of itself, forces us to probe much more deeply into the entire question of ministerial education in the Church.

Sacramental ministry and theological education

Since Trent the Church has insisted on forming and educating its ministers in its own professional academies. It hoped that this process would continue through the minister's personal initiative within his structured and clerical life. The Church trained its ministers for a life it rigidly controlled. But the further recruitment of young and generous men in order to shape them in the mould of clerical life as it is still described by the Vatican Council will soon border on the immoral. At the moment it seems highly irresponsible to continue the preparation of men for a disappearing profession.

This does not mean that Christian ministry will require less intellectual formation. But this latter can develop only on the condition of a better and more general Christian education. The problem here is that this term has become confusingly all-inclusive and thereby lost its precise meaning. It must be redefined. Personal maturity, theological precision, contemplative prayer and heroic charity are not specifically Christian. Atheists can be mature; non-Catholics, theologically precise; Buddhists, mystics and pagans heroically generous. The *specific* result of Christian education is the *sensus ecclesiae*, 'the sense of the Church'. The man joined to this is rooted in the living authority of the Church, lives the imaginative inventiveness of the faith, and expresses himself in terms of the gifts of the Spirit.

This 'sense' is the result of reading the sources of authentic Christian tradition, of participation in the prayerful celebration of the liturgy, of a distinct *way* of life. It is the fruit of experiencing Christ and the measure of prayer's real depth. It follows upon penetration of the faith's content through the light of intelligence and the force of will. When choosing an adult for the diaconate or priesthood, we shall look for this 'sense' in him, rather than accept theology credits or time spent in retreat from the world. We shall not look for professional competence to teach the public, but prophetic humility to moderate a Christian group.

I assume that weekly preparation through readings for liturgical celebration is a better formation for the exercise of ministry than specialization in theological studies. In saying this, I do not intend to underrate the importance of rigorous theological study. I only want to put it in its proper place. Ultimately, the function of theology is to clarify a contemporary statement, or verify its fidelity to revealed truth. The contemporary expression of revealed truth is only the result of the Church's faith. The function of theological science, therefore, is analogous to that of literary criticism. The *lectio divina* is akin to the savouring of literature itself. Theology verifies our fidelity; spiritual reading nourishes our faith. As the social sciences become more complex and specialized in response to the problems of technological society, so the fidelity of the Christian community increasingly depends on its competence to express the faith in a language new to the Christian, who lives in a situation never before interpreted in the light of the gospel. The Church will grow in the child-like simplicity of its faith and in the intellectual depth of its theology.

Nearly all of what is now considered theological science will pass out of the exclusive competence of the Church. Already most of the subjects of the seminary curriculum are competently taught in secular universities by men of all faiths. With the closing of the seminary the omnicompetent theological generalist will disappear. The study of theology will become oriented towards specialized research and teaching, rather than towards all-round professional performance. Christian professors who possess this 'sense' of the Church will orient students towards a biblical and ecclestical unity in their studies, a task never really accomplished by ecclesiastical curriculums.

Theological study will also become more widespread. The Christian college graduate, desiring to participate more actively in his weekly small group liturgy, will seek intellectual analysis in systematic theological reading and studies. He will have the time to do so because of the increase of leisure time in our society. Those who will have combined the asceticism leading to sexual renunciation with their years of study and liturgical participation will be uniquely fitted for the episcopacy. The Christian community will not hesitate or err in recognizing their charisma.

Increasingly the Church's teaching function will cease to express itself in pastoral letters condemning abortion and encyclicals advocating social justice. The Church will discover new faith and power in the revealed word. It will teach through a living and intimate liturgy centred around this word. Small Christian communities will be nourished in its joyful celebration.

The Spirit, continually re-creating the Church, can be trusted. Creatively present in each Christian celebration, He makes men conscious of the kingdom which lives in them. Whether composed of a few persons around the deacon, or of the Church's integral presence around the bishop, the Christian celebration renews the *whole* Church, the whole of humanity. The Church will clearly manifest the Christian faith as the progressively joyful revelation of love's *personal* meaning – the same love which all men celebrate.

[handwritten note:] This seems to presuppose a lot more "leisure" than seems to be the case for most professional men

7 The Powerless Church

In April of 1967 the secretaries for social action of the
Anglican church met for a consultation. I was invited to
attend. Dozens of social issues were on the table, and on some
there was more than one conflicting position. I had the
impression that on each issue the assembly made an effort to
determine which position could be labelled the Christian one,
and if this failed, tried at least to designate one as more
Christian than the other.

One of my contributions to this conference was the address
which follows. It concerns the role of the church in social
change and development.

It is my thesis that only the Church can 'reveal' to us the full meaning of development. To live up to this task the Church must recognize that she is growing powerless to orient or produce development. The less efficient she is as a power the more effective she can be as a celebrant of the mystery.

This statement, if understood, is resented equally by the hierarch who wants to justify collections by increasing his service to the poor, and by the rebel priest who wants to use his collar as an attractive banner in agitation. Both make a living off the social service the Church renders. In my mind both symbolize obstacles to the specific function of the Church: the annunciation of the gospel.

This specific function of the Church must be a contribution to development which could not be made by any other institution. I believe that this contribution is faith in Christ. Applied to development, faith in Christ means the revelation that the development of humanity tends towards the realization of the kingdom, which is Christ already present in the Church. The Church interprets to modern man development as a growth into Christ. She introduces him to the contemplation of this mystery in prayer and to its celebration in her liturgy.

I believe that the specific task of the Church in the modern world is the Christian celebration of the experience of change. In order to fulfil this task the Church will have to renounce progressively the 'power to do good' she now has, and see this power pass into the hands of a new type of institution: the voluntary and ever controversial embodiments of secular religion.

Later I will explain what I mean by the progressive renunciation of power and the growth of secular religion. Here I wish to explain what I mean by the celebration of change.

We have ceased to live against a rigid framework. All-enveloping, penetrating change is the fundamental experience of our age, which comes as a shock to those brought up in a different age.

In the past the same experience was exceptional and had many appearances: exile ... migration ... imprisonment ... overseas assignment ... education ... hospitalization. All these traditionally represent the sudden loss of the environment which had given form to a man's feelings and concepts. This experience of change is now faced as a lifelong process by every individual in technological society.

In Cuernavaca we have set up a centre at which we train persons to feel with others what change means to their hearts. What happens to the intimacy of a person when his familiar surroundings suddenly disappear, and with them the symbols he reveres? What happens when the words into which he was taught to pour the stream of his life lose their accustomed meaning?

What happens to the feelings of a mountain Indian thrown into a factory? What anguish does the Chicago missionary feel when he is suddenly exposed to the mountains of Bolivia, and finds himself used as a cover-up for napalm bombs? What happens to the heart of a nun who leaves the convent?

These questions are precise and elusive: each must be fitted to the one heart it opens.

What threat and what challenge does social change represent to this individual or to that social group? How does this heart or that common mood react to a change in setting? We speak about threat and about challenge because the reaction to transition is very ambiguous. It can allow for new insights, can open new perspectives and therefore confront the person with new awareness of choice. In other words, development can be a setting for salvation which leads to resurrection. But also transition can reduce a bewildered individual to a defensive self-centredness, to dependence and aggression; it can lead into the agony of a lived destruction of life, straight into hell.

Neither efficiency nor comfort nor affluence is a criterion for the quality of change. Only the reaction of the human heart to change indicates the objective value of that change. All measures of change which disregard the response of the human heart are either evil or naïve. Development is not judged against a rule but against an experience. And this experience is not available through the study of tables but through the celebration of shared experience: dialogue, controversy, play, poetry – in short, self-realization in creative leisure.

The Church teaches us to discover the transcendental meaning of this experience of life. She teaches us in liturgical celebration to recognize the presence of Christ in the growing mutual relatedness which results from the complexity and specialization of development. And she reveals to us the personal responsibility for our sins: our growing dependence, solitude and cravings which result from our self-alienation in things and systems and heroes. She challenges us to deeper poverty instead of security in achievements; personalization of love (chastity) instead of depersonalization by idolatry; faith in the other rather than prediction.

Thus the Church does not orient change, or teach how to react to it. It opens a new dimension of specific faith to an ecumenical experience of transcendent humanism. All men experience life – the Christian believes he has discovered its meaning.

What the Church contributes through evangelization is like the laughter in the joke. Two hear the same story – but one gets the point. It is like the rhythm in the phrase which only the poet catches.

The new era of constant development must not only be enjoyed, it must be brought about. What is the task of the Church in the gestation of the new world?

The Church can accelerate time by celebrating its advent, but it is not the Church's task to engineer its shape. She must resist that temptation. Otherwise she cannot celebrate the wondrous surprise of the coming, the advent.

The future has already broken into the present. We each live in many times. The present of one is the past of another, and the future of yet another. We are called to live knowing that the future exists, and that it is shared when it is celebrated. The change which has to be brought about can only be lived. We cannot plan our way to humanity. Each one of us and each of the groups with which we live and work must become a model of the era we desire to create. The many models which will develop should give to each one of us an environment in which we celebrate our creative response to change with others who need us.

Let the Church be courageous enough to lead us in the celebration by highlighting its depth. Let the Church discern the spirit of God wherever charismatic gifts call the future into the present and thus create a model to live.

Let the Church be *mater et magistra* of this play – accentuate its beauty; let her teach us to live change because it is enriching and joyful, and not just produce it because it is useful.

Awareness of change heightens the sense of personal responsibility to share its benefits. Awareness of change therefore does not only lead to a call to celebration but also to a call to work; to the elimination of obstacles which make it impossible for others to free themselves from toil and illusion.

Social change always implies a change of social structure, a change of formalized values, and finally a change of social character. These three factors constrain invention and creativity, and action against these constraints becomes a responsibility of those who experience them as shackles. Hence, social change involves a triple reaction:

1. The reorganization of social structure, which is felt as subversion or revolution.

2. The attempt to get beyond public illusions which justify structures, which implies the ridicule of ideologies and is felt as ungodliness or as education.

3. The emergence of a new 'social character', which is experienced by many with utter confusion and anguish.

Throughout history the Church has participated constantly in the shaping of social change: either as a force of conservation or as a force of social promotion. She has blessed governments and condemned them. She has justified systems and declared them as unholy. She has recommended thrift and bourgeois values and declared them anathema.

We believe that now the moment has come for the Church to withdraw from specific social initiative – taken in the name of Church structure. Let us follow the example of the Pope: have the courage to allow churchmen to make statements so ephemeral that they could never be construed as being the Church's teaching.

This withdrawal is very painful. The reason is precisely that the Church still has so much power – which has so often been used for evil. Some now argue that, given the power, it should now be used to make amends.

If the Church at present in Latin America does not use the power she has accumulated for fundamental education, labour organization, cooperative promotion, political orientation, she leaves herself open to criticism – from without, of creating a power vacuum; and from within, in the terms of 'if anybody, the Church can bear having power, because she is self-critical enough to renounce its abuse!'

But if the Church uses the power basis she has – for example, in the field of education – then she perpetuates her inability to witness to that which is specific in her mission.

Social innovation is becoming an increasingly complex process. Innovative action must be taken with increasing frequency and sophistication. This requires men who are courageous, dedicated, willing to lose their careers. I believe that this innovative action will increasingly be taken by groups committed to radically humanist ideals, and not gospel authority, and should therefore not be taken by Churches.

The modern humanist does not need the gospel as a norm; the Christian wants to remain free to find through the gospel a dimension of effective surprise beyond and above the humanistic reason which motivated social action.

The social-action group needs operational freedom: the freedom to let convenience or opportunism dictate the choice of priorities of objectives, tactics and even strategy. The same social goal might be intended by two opposed groups, one choosing violence as a method, the other non-violence.

Social action by necessity divides tactical opponents. But if organized around deeply held, radically human, ideological tenets, it also acts as a powerful catalyst for new forms of secular ecumenicism: the ecumenicism of action springing from common radical conviction.

Ideological tenets generate secular–religious, civic–religious ideas. Social action organized around such ideas, therefore, frees the Church from the age-old dilemma of risking its unity in the celebration of faith in favour of its *service* to controversial charity.

The Christian response has been deeply affected by the acceleration of time; by change, development, by growth having become normal and permanence the exception. Formerly the king could be at the opposite pole from the priest, the sacred from the profane, the churchly from the secular, and we could speak about the impact which one would have on the other.

We stand at the end of a century-long struggle to free man from the constraint of ideologies, persuasions and religions as guiding forces in his life. A non-thematic awareness of the significance of the incarnation emerges: an ability to say one great 'Yes' to the experience of life.

A new polarity emerges: a day-by-day insight into the tension between the manipulation of things and the relationship to persons.

We become capable of affirming the autonomy of the ludicrous in face of the useful, of the gratuitous as opposed to the purposeful, of the spontaneous as opposed to the rationalized and planned, of creative expression made possible by inventive solution.

We will need ideological rationalizations for a long time to achieve purposefully planned inventive solutions to social problems. Let consciously secular ideology assume this task.

I want to celebrate my faith for no purpose at all.

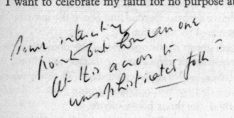

8 The Futility of Schooling

To provide every citizen in the United States with a level of schooling now enjoyed by the well-off one-third would require the addition of forty thousand million dollars per year to the present cost of elementary and secondary education in the United States, which is about thirty-seven thousand million. This sum exceeds the present expenditure for the war in Vietnam. Evidently the United States is too poor to provide compensatory education on this scale. And yet it is politically inexpedient and intellectually disreputable to question the elusive goal of providing equal educational opportunities for all citizens by giving them access to an equal number of years in school.

One man's illusions are often best recognized in the light of another man's delusions. My discussion of the futility of schooling in the Third World – published as a magazine article in 1968 – may help to demonstrate the general futility of world-wide educational institutions.

For the past two decades, demographic considerations have coloured all discussion about development in Latin America. In 1950 some 200 million people occupied the area extending from Mexico to Chile. Of these, 120 million lived directly or indirectly on primitive agriculture. Assuming both effective population controls and the most favourable possible results from programmes aimed at the increase of agriculture, by 1985 forty million people will produce most of the food for a total population of 360 million. The remaining 320 million will be either marginal to the economy or will have to be incorporated somehow into urban living and industrial production.

During these same past twenty years, both Latin American governments and foreign technical-assistance agencies have come to rely increasingly on the capacity of grammar, trade and high schools to lead the non-rural majority out of its marginality in shanty towns and subsistence farms into the type of factory, market and public forum which corresponds to modern technology. It was assumed that schooling would eventually produce a broad middle class with values resembling those of highly industrialized nations, despite the economy of continued scarcity.

Accumulating evidence now indicates that schooling does not and cannot produce the expected results. Some years ago the governments of the Americas joined in an Alliance for Progress, which has, in practice, served mainly the progress of the middle classes in the Latin nations. In most countries the Alliance has encouraged the replacement of a closed, feudal, hereditary elite by one which is supposedly 'meritocratic' and open to the few who manage to finish school. Concomitantly, the urban service proletariat has grown at several times the rate of the traditional landless rural mass and has replaced it in importance. The marginal majority and the schooled minority grow ever further apart. One old feudal society has brought forth two classes, separate and unequal.

This development has led to educational research focused on the improvement of the learning process in schools and on the adaptations of schools themselves to the special circumstances prevailing in underdeveloped societies. But logic would seem to require that we do not stop with an effort to improve schools; rather that we question the assumption on which the school system itself is based. We must not exclude the possibility that the emerging nations cannot be schooled, that schooling is not a viable answer to their need for universal education. Perhaps this type of insight is needed to clear the way for a futuristic scenario in which schools as we know them today would disappear.

The social distance between the growing urban mass and the new elite is a new phenomenon, unlike the traditional forms of discrimination known in Latin America. This new discrimination is not a transitory thing which can be overcome by schooling. On the contrary: I submit that one of the reasons for the awakening frustration in the majorities is the progressive acceptance of the 'liberal myth', the assumption that schooling is an assurance of social integration.

The solidarity of all citizens based on their common graduation from school has been an inalienable part of the modern, Western self-image. Colonization has not succeeded in implanting this myth equally in all countries, but everywhere schooling has become the prerequisite for membership in a managerial middle class. The constitutional history of Latin America since its independence has made the masses of this continent particularly susceptible to the conviction that all citizens have a right to enter – and, therefore, have some possibility of entering – their society through the door of a school.

More than elsewhere, in Latin America the teacher as missionary for the school-gospel has found adherents at the grass-roots. Only a few years ago many of us were happy when finally the Latin American school system was singled out as the area of privileged investment for international assistance funds. In fact, during the past years, both national budgets and private investment have been stimulated to increase educational allocations. But as second look reveals that this school system has built a narrow bridge across a widening social gap. As the only legitimate passage to the middle class, the school restricts all unconventional crossings and leaves the underachiever to bear the blame for his marginality.

This statement is difficult for Americans to understand. In the United States, the nineteenth-century persuasion that free schooling ensures all citizens equality in the economy and effective participation in the society survives. It is by no means certain that the result of schooling ever measured up to this expectation, but the schools certainly played a more prominent role in this process some hundred years ago.

In the United States of the mid-nineteenth century, six years of schooling frequently made a young man the educational superior of his book. In a society largely dominated by unschooled achievers, the little red schoolhouse was an effective road to social equality. A few years in school for all brought most extremes together. Those who achieved power and money without schooling had to accept a degree of equality with those who achieved literacy and did not strike it rich. Computers, television and aeroplanes have changed this. Today in Latin America, in the midst of modern technology, three times as many years of schooling and twenty times as much money as was then spent on grammar schools will not produce the same social result. The dropout from the sixth grade is unable to find a job even as a punch-card operator or a railroad hand.

Contemporary Latin America needs school systems no more than it needs railroad tracks. Both – spanning continents – served to speed the now-rich and established nations into the industrial age. Both, if now handled with care, are harmless heirlooms from the Victorian period. But neither is relevant to countries emerging from primitive agriculture directly into the jet age. Latin America cannot afford to maintain outmoded social institutions amid modern technological processes.

By 'school' of course, I do not mean all organized formal education. I use the term 'school' and 'schooling' here to designate a form of child care and a *rite de passage* which we take for granted. We forget that this institution and the corresponding creed appeared on the scene only with the growth of the industrial state. Comprehensive schooling today involves year-round, obligatory and universal classroom attendance in small groups for several hours each day. It is imposed on all citizens for a period of ten to eighteen years. School divides life into two segments, which are increasingly of comparable length. As much as anything else, schooling implies custodial care for persons who are declared undesirable elsewhere by the simple fact that a school has been built to serve them. The school is supposed to take the excess population from the street, the family or the labour force. Teachers are given the power to invent new criteria according to which new segments of the population may be committed to a school. This restraint on healthy, productive and potentially independent human beings is performed by schools with an economy which only labour camps could rival.

Schooling also involves a process of accepted ritual certification for all members of a 'schooled' society. Schools select those who are bound to succeed and send them on their way with a badge marking them fit. Once universal schooling has been accepted as the hallmark for the in-members of a society, fitness is measured by the amount of time and money spent on formal education in youth rather than ability acquired independently from an 'accredited' curriculum.

A first important step toward radical educational reform in Latin America will be taken when the educational system of the United States is accepted for what it is: a recent, imaginative social invention perfected since the Second World War and historically rooted in the American frontier. The creation of the all-pervasive school establishment, tied into industry, government and the military, is an invention no less original than the guild-centred apprenticeship of the Middle Ages, or the *doctrina de los indios* and the *reducción* of Spanish missionaries in Mexico and Paraguay, respectively, or the *lycée* and *les grandes écoles* in France. Each one of these systems was produced by its society to give stability to an achievement; each has been heavily pervaded by ritual to which society bowed; and each has been rationalized into an all-embracing persuasion, religion or ideology. The United States is not the first nation that has been willing to pay a high price to have its educational system exported by missionaries to all corners of the world. The colonization of Latin America by the catechism is certainly a noteworthy precedent.

It is difficult now to challenge the school as a system because we are so used to it. Our industrial categories tend to define results as products of specialized institutions and intruments. Armies produce defence for countries. Churches procure salvation in an afterlife. Binet defined intelligence as that which his tests test. Why not, then, conceive of education as the product of schools? Once this tag has been accepted, unschooled education gives the impression of something spurious, illegitimate and certainly unaccredited.

For some generations, education has been based on massive schooling, just as security was based on massive retaliation and, at least in the United States, transportation on the family car. The United States, because it industrialized earlier, is rich enough to afford schools, the Strategic Air Command, and the car – no matter what the toll. Most nations of the world are not that rich; they behave, however, as if they were. The example of nations which 'made it' leads Brazilians to pursue the ideal of the family car – just for a few. It compels Peruvians to squander on Mirage bombers – just for a show. And it drives every government in Latin America to spend up to two-fifths of its total budget on schools, and to do so unchallenged.

Let us insist, for a moment, on this analogy between the school system and the system of transportation based on the family car. Ownership of a car is now rapidly becoming the ideal in Latin America – at least among those who have a voice in formulating national goals. During the past twenty years, roads, parking facilities and services for private automobiles have been immensely improved. These improvements benefit overwhelmingly those who have their own cars – that is, a tiny percentage. The bias of the budget allocated for transportation thus discriminates against the best transportation for the greatest number – and the huge capital investments in this area ensure that this bias is here to stay. In some countries, articulate minorities now challenge the family car as the fundamental unit of transportation in emerging societies. But everywhere in Latin America it would be political suicide to advocate radical limitations on the multiplication of schools. Opposition parties may challenge at times the need for superhighways or the need for weapons which will see active duty only in a parade. But what man in his right mind would challenge the need to provide every child with a chance to go to high school?

Before poor nations could reach this point of universal schooling, however, their ability to educate would be exhausted. Even ten or twelve years of schooling are beyond 85 per cent of all men of our century if they happen to live outside the tiny islands where capital accumulates. Nowhere in Latin America do 27 per cent of any age group get beyond the sixth grade, nor do more than 1 per cent graduate from a university. Yet no government spends less than 18 per cent of its budget on schools, and many spend more than 30 per cent. Universal schooling, as this concept has been defined recently in industrial societies, is obviously beyond their means. The annual cost of schooling a United States citizen between the ages of twelve and twenty-four equals as much as most Latin Americans earn in two or three years.

Schools will stay beyond the means of the developing nations: neither radical population control nor maximum reallocations of government budgets nor unprecedented foreign aid would end the present unfeasibility of school systems aimed at twelve years of schooling for all. Population control needs time to become effective when the total population is as young as that of tropical America. The percentage of the world's resources invested in schooling cannot be raised beyond certain levels, nor can this budget grow beyond foreseeable maximal rates. Finally, foreign aid would have to increase to 30 per cent of the receiving nation's national budget to provide effectively for schooling, a goal not to be anticipated.

Furthermore, the per capita cost of schooling itself is rising everywhere as schools accept those who are difficult to teach, as retention rates rise, and as the quality of schooling itself improves. This rise in cost neutralizes much of the new investments. Schools do not come cheaper by the dozen.

In view of all these factors, increases in school budgets must usually be defended by arguments which imply default. In fact, however, schools are untouchable because they are vital to the *status quo*. Schools have the effect of tempering the subversive potential of education in an alienated society because, if education is confined to schools, only those who have been schooled into compliance on a lower grade are admitted to its higher reaches. In capital-starved societies not rich enough to purchase unlimited schooling, the majority is schooled not only into compliance but also into subservience.

Since Latin American constitutions were written with an eye on the United States, the ideal of universal schooling was a creative utopia. It was a condition necessary to create the Latin American nineteenth-century bourgeoisie. Without the pretence that every citizen has a right to go to school, the liberal bourgeoisie could never have developed; neither could the middle-class masses of present-day Europe, the United States and Russia, nor the managerial middle elite of their cultural colonies in South America. But the same school which worked in the last century to overcome feudalism has now become an oppressive idol which protects those who are already schooled. Schools grade and, therefore, they degrade. They make the degraded accept his own submission. Social seniority is bestowed according to the level of schooling achieved. Everywhere in Latin America more money for schools means more privilege for a few at the cost of most, and this patronage of an elite is explained as a political ideal. This ideal is written into laws which state the patently impossible: equal scholastic opportunities for all.

The number of satisfied clients who graduate from schools every year is much smaller than the number of frustrated drop-outs who are conveniently graded by their failure for use in a marginal labour pool. The resulting steep educational pyramid defines a rationale for the corresponding levels of social status. Citizens are 'schooled' into their places. This results in politically acceptable forms of discrimination which benefit the relatively few achievers.

The move from the farm to the city in Latin America still frequently means a move from a world where status is explained as a result of inheritance into a world where it is explained as a result of schooling. Schools allow a head start to be rationalized as an achievement. They give to privilege not only the appearance of equality but also of generosity: should somebody who missed out on early schooling be dissatisfied with the status he holds, he can always be referred to a night or trade school. If he does not take advantage of such recognized remedies, his exclusion from privilege can be explained as his own fault. Schools temper the frustrations they provoke.

The school system also inculcates its own universal acceptance. Some schooling is not necessarily more education than none, especially in a country where every year a few more people can get all the schooling they want while most people never complete the sixth grade. But much less than six years seems to be sufficient to inculcate in the child the acceptance of the ideology which goes with the school grade. The child learns only about the superior status and unquestioned authority of those who have more schooling than he has.

Any discussion or radical alternatives to school-centred formal education upsets our notions of society. No matter how inefficient schools are in educating a majority, no matter how effective schools are in limiting the access to the elite, no matter how liberally schools shower their non-educational benefits on the members of this elite, schools do increase the national income. They qualify their graduates for more economic production. In an economy on the lower rungs of development toward United States-type industrialization, a school graduate is enormously more productive than a dropout. Schools are part and parcel of a society in which a minority is on the way to becoming so productive that the majority must be schooled into disciplined consumption. Schooling therefore – under the best of circumstances – helps to divide society into two groups: those so productive that their expectation of annual rise in personal income lies far beyond the national average, and the overwhelming majority whose income also rises, but at a rate clearly below the former's. These rates, of course, are compounded and lead the two groups further apart.

Radical innovation in formal education presupposes radical political changes, radical changes in the organization of production, and radical changes in man's image of himself as an animal which needs school. This is often forgotten when sweeping reforms of the schools are proposed and fail because of the societal framework we accept. For instance, the trade school is sometimes advocated as a cure-all for mass schooling. Yet it is doutful that the products of trade schools would find employment in a continuously changing, ever more automated economy. Moreover the capital and operating costs of trade schools, as we know them today, are several times as high as those for a standard school of the same grade. Also, trade schools usually take in sixth graders, who, as we have seen, are already the exception. Trade schools pretend to educate by creating a spurious facsimile of the factory within a school building.

Instead of the trade school, we should think of a subsidized transformation of the industrial plant. It should be possible to obligate factories to serve as training centres during off-hours, for managers to spend part of their time planning and supervising this training, and for the industrial process to be so redesigned that it has educational value. If the expenditures for present schools were partly allocated to sponsor this kind of educational exploitation of existing resources, then the final results – both economic and educational – might be incomparably greater. If, further, such subsidized apprenticeship were offered to all who ask for it, irrespective of age, and not only to those who are destined to be employees in the particular plant, industry would have begun to assume an important role now played by school. We would be on the way to disabuse ourselves of the idea that manpower qualification must precede employment, that schooling must precede productive work. There is no reason for us to continue the medieval tradition in which men are prepared for the 'secular world' by incarceration in a sacred precinct, be it monastery, synagogue or school.

A second, frequently discussed, remedy for the failure of schools is fundamental, or adult, education. It has been proved by Paulo Freire in Brazil that those adults who can be interested in political issues of their community can be made literate within six weeks of evening classes. The programme teaching such reading and writing skills, of course, must be built around the emotion-loaded key words of the adults' political vocabulary. Understandably this fact has got Freire's programme into trouble. It has also been suggested that the dollar-cost of ten separate months of adult education is equal that of one year of early schooling, and can be incomparably more effective than schooling at its best.

Unfortunately, 'adult education' now is conceived principally as a device to give the 'underprivileged' a palliative for the schooling he lacks. The situation would have to be reversed if we wanted to conceive of all education as an exercise in adulthood. We should consider a radical reduction of the length of the formal, obligatory school sessions to only two months each year – but spread this type of formal schooling over the first twenty or thirty years of a man's life.

While various forms of in-service apprenticeship in factories and programmed maths and language teaching could assume a large proportion of what we have previously called 'instruction', two months a year of formal schooling should be considered ample time for what the Greeks meant by *scholè* – leisure for the pursuit of insight. No wonder we find it nearly impossible to conceive of comprehensive social changes in which the educational functions of schools would thus be redistributed in new patterns among institutions we do not now envisage. We find it equally difficult to indicate concrete ways in which the non-educational functions of a vanishing school system would be redistributed. We do not know what to do with those whom we now label 'children' or 'students' and commit to school.

It is difficult to foresee the political consequences of changes as fundamental as those proposed, not to mention the international consequences. How should a school-reared society coexist with one which has gone 'off the school standard', and whose industry, commerce, advertising and participation in politics is different as a matter of principle? Areas which develop outside the universal school standard would lack the common language and criteria for respectful coexistence with the schooled. Two such worlds, such as China and the United States, might almost have to seal themselves off from each other.

Rashly, the school-bred mind abhors the educational devices available to these worlds. It is difficult mentally to 'accredit' Mao's party as an educational institution which might prove more effective than the schools are at their best – at least when it comes to inculcating citizenship. Guerrilla warfare in Latin America is another education device much more frequently misused or misunderstood than applied. Che Guevara, for instance, clearly saw it as a last educational resort to teach a people about the illegitimacy of their political system. Especially in unschooled countries, where the transistor radio has come to every village, we must never underrate the educational functions of great charismatic dissidents like Dom Helder Camara in Brazil or Camilo Torres in Colombia. Castro described his early charismatic harangues as 'teaching sessions'.

The schooled mind perceives these processes exclusively as political indoctrination, and their educational purpose eludes its grasp. The legitimation of education by schools tends to render all non-school education an accident, if not an outright misdemeanor. And yet it is surprising with what difficulty the school-bred mind perceives the rigour with which schools inculcate their own presumed necessity, and with it the supposed inevitability of the system they sponsor. Schools indoctrinate the child into the acceptance of the political system his teachers represent, despite the claim that teaching is non-political.

Ultimately the cult of schooling will lead to violence, as the establishment of *any* religion has led to it. If the gospel of universal schooling is permitted to spread in Latin America, the military's ability to repress insurgency must grow. Only force will ultimately control the insurgency inspired by the frustrated expectation that the propagation of the school-myth enkindles. The maintenance of the present school system may turn out to be an important step on the way to Latin American fascism. Only fanaticism inspired by idolatry of a system can ultimately rationalize the massive discrimination which will result from another twenty years of grading a capital-starved society by school marks.

The time has come to recognize the real burden of the schools in the emerging nations, so that we may become free to envisage change in the social structure which now makes schools a necessity. I do not advocate a sweeping utopia like the Chinese commune for Latin America. But I do suggest that we plunge our imagination into the construction of scenarios which would allow a bold reallocation of educational functions among industry, politics, short scholastic retreats and intensive preparation of parents for providing early childhood education. The cost of schools must be measured not only in economic, social and educational terms, but in political terms as well. Schools, in an economy of scarcity invaded by automation, accentuate and rationalize the coexistence of two societies, one a colony of the other.

Once it is understood that the cost of schooling is not inferior to the cost of chaos, we might be on the brink of courageously costly compromise. Today it is as dangerous in Latin America to question the myth of social salvation through schooling as it was three hundred years ago to question the divine rights of the Catholic kings.

9 School: The Sacred Cow

Only if we understand the school system as the central myth-making ritual of industrial societies can we explain the deep need for it, the complex myth surrounding it, and the inextricable way in which schooling is tied into the self-image of contemporary man. A graduation speech at the University of Puerto Rico in Río Piedras provided me with an opportunity to probe this relationship.

This is a time of crisis in the institution of the school, a crisis which may mark the end of the 'age of schooling' in the Western world. I speak of the 'age of schooling' in the sense in which we are accustomed to speak of the 'feudal age' or of the 'Christian era'. The 'age of schooling' began about two hundred years ago. Gradually the idea grew that schooling was a necessary means of becoming a useful member of society. It is the task of this generation to bury that myth.

Your own situation is paradoxical. At the end and as a result of your studies, you are enabled to see that the education your children deserve, and will demand, requires a revolution in the school system of which you are a product.

The graduation rite that we solemnly celebrate today confirms the prerogatives which Puerto Rican society, by means of a costly system of subsidized public schools, confers upon the sons and daughters of its most privileged citizens. You are part of the most privileged 10 per cent of your generation, part of that minuscule group which has completed university studies. Public investment in each of you is fifteen times the educational investment in the average member of the poorest 10 per cent of the population, who drops out of school before completing the fifth grade.

The certificate you receive today attests to the legitimacy of your competence. It is not available to the self-educated, to those who have acquired competence by means not officially recognized in Puerto Rico. The programmes of the University of Puerto Rico are all duly accredited by the Middle States Association of Colleges and Secondary Schools.

The degree which the university today confers upon you implies that over the last sixteen years or more your elders have obliged you to submit yourselves, voluntarily or involuntarily, to the discipline of this complex scholastic rite. You have in fact been daily attendants, five days a week, nine months a year, within the sacred precinct of the school and have continued such attendance year after year, usually without interruption. Governmental and industrial employees and the professional associations have good reasons to believe that you will not subvert the order to which you have faithfully submitted in the course of completing your 'rites of initiation'.

Much of your youth has been spent within the custody of the school. It is expected that you will now go forth to work, to guarantee to future generations the privileges conferred upon you.

Puerto Rico is the only society in the Western hemisphere to devote 30 per cent of its governmental budget to education. It is one of six places in the world which devote between 6 and 7 per cent of national income to education. The schools of Puerto Rico cost more and provide more employment than any other public sector. In no other social activity is so large a proportion of the total population of Puerto Rico involved.

A huge number of people are observing this occasion on television. Its solemnity will, on the one hand, confirm their sense of educational inferiority, and on the other, raise their hopes, largely doomed to disappointment, of one day themselves receiving a university degree.

Puerto Rico has been schooled. I don't say educated but, rather, schooled. Puerto Ricans can no longer conceive of life without reference to the school. The desire for education has actually given way to the compulsion of schooling. Puerto Rico has adopted a new religion. Its doctrine is that education is a product of the school, a product which can be defined by numbers. There are the numbers which indicate how many years a student has spent under the tutelage of teachers, and others which represent the proportion of his correct answers in an examination. Upon the receipt of a diploma the educational product acquires a market value. School attendance in itself thus guarantees inclusion in the membership of disciplined consumers of the technocracy – just as in past times church attendance guaranteed membership in the community of saints. From governor to *jíbaro*, Puerto Rico now accepts the ideology of its teachers as it once accepted the theology of its priests. The school is now identified with education as the Church once was with religion.

Today's agencies of accreditation are reminiscent of the royal patronage formerly accorded the Church. Federal support of education now parallels yesterday's royal donations to the Church. The power of the diploma has grown so rapidly in Puerto Rico that the poor blame their misery on precisely the lack of that which assures to you, today's graduates, participation in society's privileges and powers.

Research shows that twice as many high-school graduates in Puerto Rico as in the States want to pursue university studies; while the probability of graduating from college for the Puerto Rican high-school graduate is much lower than it would be in the States. This widening discrepancy between aspirations and resources can result only in a deepening frustration among the inhabitants of the Island.

The later a Puerto Rican child drops out of school the more keenly does he feel his failure. Contrary to popular opinion, increasing emphasis on schooling has actually increased class conflict in Puerto Rico, and has also increased the sense of inferiority which Puerto Ricans suffer in relation to the United States.

Upon your generation falls the obligation of developing for Puerto Rico an educational process radically different from that of the present and independent of the example of other societies. It is yours to question whether Puerto Rico really wants to transform itself irrevocably into a passive product of the teaching profession. It is yours to decide whether you will subject your children to a school that seeks respectability in North American accreditation, its justification in the qualification of the labour force, and its function in permitting the children of the middle class to keep up with the Joneses of Westchester County, New York.

The real sacred cow in Puerto Rico is the school. Proponents of commonwealth, statehood and independence all take it for granted. Actually, none of these political alternatives can liberate a Puerto Rico which continues to put its primary faith in schooling. Thus, if this generation wants the true liberation of Puerto Rico, it will have to invent educational alternatives which put an end to the 'age of schooling'. This will be a difficult task. Schooling has developed a formidable folklore. The begowned academic professors whom we have witnessed today evoke the ancient procession of clerics and little angels on the day of Corpus Christi. The Church, holy, catholic, apostolic, is rivalled by the school, accredited, compulsory, untouchable, universal. Alma Mater has replaced Mother Church. The power of the school to rescue the denizen of the slum is as the power of the Church to save the Muslim Moor from hell. (Gehenna meant both slum and hell in Hebrew.) The difference between Church and school is mainly that the rites of the school have now beome much more rigorous and onerous than were the rites of the Church in the worst days of the Spanish Inquisition.

The school has become the established Church of secular times. The modern school had its origins in the impulse towards universal schooling, which began two centuries ago as an attempt to incorporate everyone into the industrial state. In the industrial metropolis the school was the integrating institution. In the colonies the school inculcated the dominant classes with the values of the imperial power and confirmed in the masses their sense of inferiority to this schooled elite. Neither the nation nor the industry of the precybernetic era can be imagined without universal baptism into the school. The dropout of this era corresponds to the lapsed marrano of eleventh-century Spain.

We have, I hope, outlived the era of the industrial state. We shall not live long, in any case, if we do not replace the anachronism of national sovereignty, industrial autarchy and cultural narcissism – which are combined into a stew of leftovers by the schools. Only within their sacred precincts could such old potage be served to young Puerto Ricans.

I hope that your grandchildren will live in an Island where the majority give as little importance to attending class as is now given to attending the Mass. We are still far from this day and I hope that you will take the responsibility for bringing it to pass without fear of being damned as heretics, subversives or ungrateful creatures. It may comfort you to know that those who undertake the same responsibility in socialist lands will be similarly denounced.

Many controversies divide our Puerto Rican society. Natural resources are threatened by industrialization, the cultural heritage is adulterated by commercialization, dignity is subverted by publicity, imagination by the violence which characterizes the mass media. Each of these is a theme for extensive public debate. There are those who want less industry, less English and less Coca-Cola, and those who want more. All agree that Puerto Rico needs many more schools.

This is not to say that education is not discussed in Puerto Rico. Quite the contrary. It would be difficult to find a society whose political and industrial leaders are as concerned with education. They all want more education, directed towards the sector which they represent. These controversies merely serve, however, to strengthen public opinion in the scholastic ideology which reduces education to a combination of classrooms, curricula, funds, examinations and grades.

I expect that by the end of this century, what we now call school will be a historical relic, developed in the time of the railroad and the private automobile and discarded along with them. I feel sure that it will soon be evident that the school is as marginal to education as the witch doctor is to public health.

A divorce of education from schooling is, in my opinion, already on the way, speeded by three forces: the Third World, the ghettos and the universities. Among the nations of the Third World, schooling discriminates against the majority and disqualifies the self-educated. Many members of the 'black' ghettos see the schools as a 'whitening' agent. Protesting university students tell us that school bores them and stands between them and reality. These are caricatures, no doubt, but the mythology of schooling makes it difficult to perceive the underlying realities.

The criticism today's students are making of their teachers is as fundamental as that which their grandfathers made of the clergy. The divorce of education from schooling has its model in the demythologizing of the church. We fight now, in the name of education, against a teaching profession which unwillingly constitutes an economic interest, as in times past the reformers fought against a clergy which was, often unwillingly, a part of the ancient power elite. Participation in a 'production system', of no matter what kind, has always threatened the prophetic function of the Church as it now threatens the educational function of the school.

School protest has deeper causes than the pretexts enunciated by its leaders. These, although frequently political, are expressed as demands for various reforms of the system. They would never have gained mass support, however, if students had not lost faith and respect in the institution which nurtured them. Student strikes reflect a profound intuition widely shared among the younger generation: the intuition that schooling has vulgarized education, that the school has become anti-educational and anti-social, as in other epochs the Church has become anti-Christian or Israel idolatrous. This intuition can, I believe, be explicitly and briefly formulated.

The protest of some students today is analogous to the dissidence of those charismatic leaders without whom the Church would never have been reformed: their prophecies led to martyrdom, their theological insights to their persecutions as heretics, their saintly activity often led to the stake. The prophet is always accused of subversion, the theologian of irreverence and the saint is written off as crazy.

The Church has always depended for its vitality upon the sensitivity of its bishops to the appeals of the faithful, who see the rigidity of the ritual as an obstacle to their faith. The churches, incapable of dialogue between their ruling clerics and their dissidents, have become museum pieces, and this could easily happen with the school system of today. It is easier for the university to attribute dissidence to ephemeral causes than to attribute this dissidence to a profound alienation of the students from the school. It is also easier for student leaders to operate with political slogans than to launch basic attacks upon sacred cows. The university that accepts the challenge of its dissident students and helps them to formulate in a rational and coherent manner the anxiety they feel because they are rejecting schooling exposes itself to the danger of being ridiculed for its supposed credulity. The student leader who tries to promote in his companions the consciousness of a profound aversion to their school (not to education itself) finds that he creates a level of anxiety which few of his followers care to face.

The university has to learn to distinguish between sterile criticism of scholastic authority and a call for the conversion of the school to the educational purposes for which it was founded, between destructive fury and the demand for radically new forms of education – scarcely conceivable by minds formed in the scholastic tradition; between, on the one hand, cynicism which seeks new benefits for the already privileged and, on the other, Socratic sarcasm, which questions the educational efficacy of accepted forms of instruction in which the institution is investing its major resources. It is necessary, in other words, to distinguish between the alienated mob and profound protest based on rejection of the school as a symbol of the *status quo*.

In no other place in Latin America has investment in education, demand for education, and information about education, increased so rapidly as in Puerto Rico. There is no place, therefore, in which members of your generation could begin the search for a new style of public education so readily as in Puerto Rico. It is up to you to get us back, recognizing that the generations which preceded you were misled in their efforts to achieve social equality by means of universal compulsory schooling.

In Puerto Rico three of every ten students drop out of school before finishing the sixth grade. This means that only one of every two children, from families with less than the median income, completes the elementary school. Thus half of all Puerto Rican parents are under a sad illusion if they believe that their children have more than an outside chance of entering the university.

Public funds for education go directly to the schools, without students having any control of them. The political justification for this practice is that it gives everyone equal access to the classroom. However, the high cost of this type of education, dictated by educators trained largely outside Puerto Rico, makes a public lie of the concept of equal access. Public schools may benefit all of the teachers but benefit mainly the few students who reach the upper levels of the system. It is precisely our insistence on direct financing of the 'free school' that causes this concentration of scarce resources on benefits for the children of the few.

I believe that every Puerto Rican has the right to receive an equal part of the educational budget. This is something very different and much more concrete than the mere promise of a place in the school. I believe, for example, that a young thirteen year old who has had only four years of schooling has much more right to the remaining educational resources than students of the same age who have had eight years of schooling. The more 'disadvantaged' a citizen is, the more he needs a guarantee of his right.

If in Puerto Rico it were decided to honour this right, then the free school would immediately have to be abandoned. The annual quota of each person of school age would obviously not support a year of schooling, at present costs. The insufficiency would, of course, be even more dramatic if the total educational budget for all levels were divided among the population from six to twenty-five years of age, the period between kindergarten and graduate studies, to which all Puerto Ricans supposedly have free access.

These facts leave us three options: leave the system as it is, at the cost of justice and conscience; use the available funds exclusively to assure free schooling to children whose parents earn less than the median income; or use the available public resources to offer to all the education that an equal share of these resources could assure to each. The better-off could, of course, supplement this amount and might continue to offer their children the doubtful privilege of participating in the process which you are completing today. The poor would certainly use their share to acquire an education more efficiently and at lower cost.

The same choices apply, *a fortiori*, to other parts of Latin America where frequently not more than twenty dollars a year in public funds would be available for each child if the 20 per cent of tax receipts now destined for education were distributed equally to all children who should be in school under existing laws. This amount could never pay for a year of conventional schooling. It would however be enough to provide a good many children and adults with one month of intensive education year after year. It would also be enough to finance the distribution of educational games leading to skills with numbers, letters and logical symbols. And to sponsor successive periods of intensive apprenticeship. In North-East Brazil, Paulo Freire (who was forced to leave the country) showed us that with a single investment of this amount he was able to educate 25 per cent of an illiterate population to the point where they could do functional reading. But this, as he made clear, was only possible when his literacy programme could focus on the key words that are politically controversial within a community.

My suggestions may mortify many. But it is from the great positivists and liberals that we inherited the principle of using public funds for the administration of schools directed by professional educators; just as, previously, tithes had been given to the Church to be administered by priests. It remains for you to fight the free public school in the name of true equality of educational opportunity. I admire the courage of those of you willing to enter this fight.

Youth wants educational institutions that provide them with education. They neither want nor need to be mothered, to be certified or to be indoctrinated. It is difficult, obviously, to get an education from a school that refuses to educate without requiring that its students submit simultaneously to custodial care, sterile competition and indoctrination. It is difficult, obviously, to finance a teacher who is at the same time regarded as guardian, umpire, counsellor and curriculum manager. It is uneconomical to combine these functions in one institution. It is precisely the fusion of these four functions, frequently antithetical, which raises the cost of education acquired in school. This is also the source of our chronic shortage of educational resources. It is up to you to create institutions that offer education to all at a cost within the limits of public resources.

Only when Puerto Rico has psychologically outgrown the school will it be able to finance education for all, and only then will truly efficient, non-scholastic forms of education find acceptance. Meanwhile, these new forms of education will have to be designed as provisional means of compensating for the failures of the schools. In order to create new forms of education, we will have to demonstrate alternatives to the school that offer preferable options to students, teachers and taxpayers.

There is no intrinsic reason why the education that schools are now failing to provide could not be acquired more successfully in the setting of the family, of work and communal activity, in new kinds of libraries and other centres that would provide the means of learning. But the institutional forms that education will take in tomorrow's society cannot be clearly visualized. Neither could any of the great reformers anticipate concretely the institutional styles that would result from their reforms. The fear that new institutions will be imperfect, in their turn, does not justify our servile acceptance of present ones.

This plea to imagine a Puerto Rico without schools must, for many of you, come as a surprise. It is precisely for surprise that true education prepares us. The purpose of public education should be no less fundamental than the purpose of the Church, although the purpose of the latter is more explicit. The basic purpose of public education should be to create a situation in which society obliges each individual to take stock of himself and his poverty. Education implies a growth of an independent sense of life and a relatedness which go hand in hand with increased access to, and use of, memories stored in the human community. The educational institution provides the focus for this process. This presupposes a place within the society in which each of us is awakened by surprise; a place of encounter in which others surprise me with their liberty and make me aware of my own. The university itself, if it is to be worthy of its traditions, must be an institution whose purposes are identified with the exercise of liberty, whose autonomy is based on public confidence in the use of that liberty.

My friends, it is your task to surprise yourselves, and us, with the education you succeed in inventing for your children. Our hope of salvation lies in our being surprised by the Other. Let us learn always to receive further surprises. I decided long ago to hope for surprises until the final act of my life – that is to say, in death itself.

10 Sexual Power and Political Potency

In urban areas of Latin America, at least one of four pregnancies terminates in abortion. In many inner city districts the rate is even higher. At the end of their childbearing age, at least two women in five have braved serious damage to their health, disrepute, and often gruesome guilt to avoid the birth of another child. All this happens in a culture in which common-law marriage and illegitimate births approach and even exceed Church marriages or legitimate births, and no stigma comparable to that known in the Anglo-Saxon world attaches to either. It also happens in a culture where other people's abandoned children are easily welcomed for upbringing in one's own family, without any formality. Evidently a lot of people do not want to have any more children.

Most of these abortions are performed by midwives, herb-doctors and witches, except in Uruguay and Argentina, where many doctors volunteer their illegal services even to the poor. Abortion is by far the most frequent cause of death among young women. These women need an alternative to the present situation.

The conditions of increased carnage are favourable. Enough girls have already been born to ensure a doubling of women of childbearing age in the very early 1980s. Neither development nor revolution can prevent growing misery for an exploding and hungry population, which drifts into abulia and passivity. It would be misleading to tell a woman seeking an abortion that a rosy future is on the horizon for her child.

But also, where can politicians afford to take a strong, positive stand for either birth control or legal abortion? Only a strong-man could afford simultaneously to date traditional Catholics who speak about sin, communists who want to out-breed the US imperialists and nationalists who speak about colonizing vast unsettled expanses.

The major change in public policy must be intitiated at the grass roots. Present programmes, semi-clandestine, try to gain acceptance for birth control among the common people. I suggest that a major campaign demanding clear population policies should rise from the grass roots. In the following article, I explain why this campaign must be coupled with a major effort leading to critically increased political awareness. This was originally a speech given at a meeting of population experts in 1967. Since it has frequently been quoted, I have left it unchanged, fully aware that my attempt to be compact makes it difficult reading.

This speech was given some months before publication of the notorious papal encyclical on birth control. I had hoped that the Pope would speak, but wagered that he would keep silent. I lost my wager, and was disappointed. I had hoped that the Pope would speak about the ambiguity of technology, as well as the need for a more intense consciousness and love on the part of men forced by circumstances to use that technology. I had hoped that the Pope would make all men face the fact that lowered infant mortality must be accompanied by equally lowered birth rates, if we wanted to avoid widespread de-humanization, and that we were obligated as Christians to restrain self-reproduction. The results of modern hygiene's fostering physical life must be countered by the use of modern hygiene to check its cancerous growth.

Instead the Pope came out with a document written in dead, juridical language, a document into which one can read all this, but one which lacks courage, is in bad taste, and takes the initiative away from Rome in the attempt to lead modern men in Christian humanism. This is sad.

In Latin America the population is exploding. The citizenry of Mexico is doubled every eighteen years, that of Brazil every seventeen and that of Peru every twenty. A swelling of the lower age groups is occurring in countries where, even now, two-thirds of youth cannot complete an elementary education. The result of this is not only inferior education for the great majority, but also the growing awareness of the adult masses that they are being excluded from all the key institutions of middle-class society. The brief education they receive is, in the long run, an education in dissatisfaction.

Birth control programmes in Latin America generally fail because they stress the fear of poverty rather than the joy of life. An individual may employ contraception as the only defence against imminent misery – or he can choose it as a constructive means for a more human life. But there is nothing constructive in the present message of family planning. It is addressed to the same audience as the TV commercial and billboard advertising: the minority that is moving into the middle class. Today's clients for consumer goods and contraceptives in Mexico and Brazil form an odd and a marginal lot; they are the very few who will allow their sexual patterns to be affected by an appeal involving constant consumption and material advancement.

Success in modern schools, in modern jobs or at modern sex seem related. Such success remains the privilege of a minority in Latin America. Although this minority is drawn from all strata of society, it is selected from those 'achievers' who know how to maintain the growth rate of their personal income above the national average. And this class of strivers surges into political power, providing further privilege to those already on their way to affluence. Even if family planning were practised by this small group, it would have little impact on the overall population growth. The 'others' (which in Latin America means most) remain excluded from an equal opportunity to plan their families. Like the legal provisions for social, educational and political equality, opportunities for the poor to practise birth control are but a mockery.

Within the present political and social context, it is impossible to induce the majority of the people to adopt birth control. Neither seduction nor current efforts at education work. To seduce effectively, the marketing of birth control would have to become more aggressive: twenty-five dollars offered for the insertion of each coil, one hundred dollars for each sterilization. To educate effectively, governments would be promoting their own subversion through sudden and widespread adult education. For it is clear that the education that enables adults to formulate their own dissent risks the loss of all constraints on freedom and imagination.

The double failure of seduction and education is based on a discrepancy between the new message and the style of life common to Latin America's peasant majorities. For most, the idea that sexual technique can prevent conception is incredible; but even less credible to them is the idea that such techniques will produce personal affluence. Both claims seem to invoke magic. Further, the style by which this magical remedy is pushed has an odious smell. It evokes a rich establishment solicitous of teaching the poor how not to reproduce their like.

Even the approach to the individual is frequently brash, involving the tragic moment in a woman's life when, as an alternative to the next abortion, she has become a receptive victim for initiation into the mystery of contraception. Claim, style and method put the accent on protection against life rather than freedom for it. No wonder they fail.

To be attractive, family planning would have to be embraced as a way to express a deeper sense of life rather than be used as a mere protection against evil.

To appeal to magic, myth and mystery must be dropped by both the proponents and the opponents of contraception. Obviously this is not easy. The vision of increasing world poverty overwhelms the imagination, and the creation of a myth is one way to escape unbearable anguish. The transformation of hungry persons into a mythical corporate enemy is as old as mankind, but so is the illusion that we can manage the myths we have made.

Once the 'poor' have been reduced to a faceless river reaching the high-water mark on a statistical table, birth-control campaigns can be credited with magical power and invoked to conjure away further flooding. Such programmes give the impression that individuals should recognize themselves as drops in a swelling tide, so that each can do his best to reduce his kind. Not surprisingly, nobody does.

Only professors can delude themselves into the belief that men can be prodded to take for their *personal motives* in family planning the possibly valid *policy reasons* of the economist and the sociologist. One's vital behaviour is always beyond the reach of a decision made by others.

Populations are mindless: they can be managed but not motivated. Only persons can make up their minds; and the more they make up their minds, the less they can be controlled. People who freely decide to control their own fertility have new motivations or aspirations to political control. It is clear that responsible parenthood cannot be separated from the quest for power in politics. Programmes that aim at such goals are unwelcome under the military governments prevailing in South America, and such programmes are not the kind usually financed by the United States.

The development of Latin America as a Western colony requires massive schooling for children, to fit them passively into the acceptance of an ideology that keeps them 'democratically' in place. Political order cannot tolerate too much awareness or originality or risk. The kind of education of adults that is analytical and dialectic leads inevitably to a liberation from taboos. Idols cannot be knocked off selectively; the kind of adult education that is aimed at dethroning some idols dethrones them all and is always politically subversive.

Kindred insights usually reinforce each other. The awareness that sex does not have to lead to unwanted motherhood provokes another concept: the insight that economic survival does not have to breed political exploitation. The freedom of the mate and of the citizen lead over the same road. Each taboo left behind means one obstacle less in the change from the social conditions that make all idols necessary.

All those who will give birth before 1984 are now in life. For each I ask: Will this child become a passive object, manipulated and sated by a technological milieu that encroaches on his feelings? Or will this child grow into a man who shares in the responsibility for a set of social trends? Will demographers trim his sex patterns to fit the planned population curve, just as industrial designers fit his job behaviour to investment needs? Or will his move from the subsistence farm to a sprawling city increase his conscious control over his own life history?

In other words, will the city swallow his life? Or will he live with deeper freedom in the city? This is the question for 300 millions. Two-thirds of the 200-odd million inhabitants of America, below the Rio Grande, now are considered 'rural'. Yet less than 35 per cent of the 350 millions expected in the next generation will make a living from agriculture. Most of those now alive – or those to be born during the next fifteen years – are existing in a world where mind, mores and myth are rooted in a rural past. This means they come from a milieu in which personal success depends on the struggle for scarce resources, say, limited land, and where survival of one's group had to be ensured by massive procreation against high mortality. Peasants value possession, tradition and multiple fertility. This taste finds expression in their style of language, symbol, ideology and religion.

Peasants' culture provides categories that endow even extreme rural privation with dignity. The individual who moves to the city loses this powerful hereditary tool, and awareness and acceptance of this loss becomes a condition for survival. This requires a change in each man: a change both of behaviour and of personal bearings.

This necessary changed in behaviour is the sum total of the change in the many strains of conduct that, like the strands of a rope, make up a human life. Each change in a man's actions (on the job, in the street or with his girl friend) is the fruit of his personal insight. Either it has freed him for the invention of a new habit, or it has resulted in his deadening submission to the new rhythm of the city.

Even more revolutionary than changed behaviour, however, are the new moorings the personality must find in the city. Urbanization for the individual means the search for new bearings in a world that assigns new coordinates to his most intimate feelings and drives. Character forces are given new labels and new slogans, and symbols are attached to them, to fit them into a new ideology.

The city, like any other engineered product, is sold to the newcomer with a set of instructions for its use. These instructions

mystify the non-believer, the man who has not subscribed to the
prevailing beliefs. This city creed has many dogmas. It prizes
a medically protracted span of life, scholastic performance and
certification, continued advancement and achievement on the
job. Production and consumption become measuring sticks for
most values, including fertility.

Change in behaviour, change in bearings and change in belief
go hand in hand. Only the few capable of this triple change can
elbow their way into the tiny islands of affluence.

Within this context, high consumption combined with high
fertility is a luxury that few can afford. These few, quite often,
are not the old bourgeois, but couples who by good luck rose
quickly and established themselves. For most families the speed
of social climb depends upon tight control of family size.

The lifelong discipline demanded by such control is hard on
any adolescent raised in a hut, untrained as he is for silent defer-
ence to the humdrum of schooling, or the monotony of an office,
or docility towards clock and schedule. A rare combination of
character, circumstances and peers is necessary to teach a peasant the set of disciplines by which he alone can ensure his climb
to the upper reaches of city, business or family life. The city is
a much better selector than teacher.

The personality structure or character that makes for a child's
success in school ensures the passing of those who will also fit the
corporate structure in the modern city. Those labelled by a
certificate and outfitted with a car are presumably those most
suited to take the needed precautions to lower their fertility and
raise their insurance. The proven correlation of high schooling
and low fertility is usually interpreted as a result of a schooling
that renders pupils capable of using technical know-how, such as
contraceptives. Actually the contrary is probable: schools select
those already inclined towards such technical know-how. This
is much more true in countries where grammar schools are selective and by that selection exclude more individuals than they
accept.

Let me explain: the height of a social pyramid in Kansas and
Caracas is about the same. What is different, north and south, is
its shape. At best, three men out of one hundred in Caracas take
the path corresponding to high-school graduation, the family car,

private health insurance and corresponding hygiene. I suggest that we distinguish between those who were lifted onto this level by birth and privilege and those who climbed there. These latter are much more carefully selected in Caracas than in Kansas. The steeper the pyramid, the more successfully it bars weakly motivated climbers who would barely even amble to the top of a slightly slanted incline. Those who scale the narrow and steep passage to success in Caracas must be sustained by more common drives and aims than those who are pushed up the broad flight of stairs of the United States college.

We are frequently reminded that family planning was adopted rapidly by certain ethnic groups, for example, Puerto Ricans in New York. Fertility of the entire group declined suddenly as the group moved to the city. This is true of those who made up their minds to go to New York and then 'made it' there: those who moved out of Harlem, through school and into jobs that pay more than $7000 annually. They are the ones who survived the police, drugs, discrimination and welfare. Indeed, they rose faster than any ethnic group before them, and their fertility, too, fell faster.

Similar groups of leapfrog immigrants to affluence can be spotted all over Latin America. Their members tend to join the Lions Club, Knights of Columbus, the Christian Family movement and other clubs that allow them to organize for further privilege for their kind. 'The Association for the Protection of the Middle Classes' recently formed by Esso employees in Caracas is a good example of their tactics. But the fact that members of such groups do control their fertility is no proof that contraception is, even partially, a result of a more comfortable life. It means more probably that at present in Latin America only a few can be bewitched by the mirage of affluence.

It is revealing that fertility among the United States poor, particularly in the black ghetto, remains near Latin American levels. The common element is not some numerical indicator but a mood. In the United States ghetto, economic averages have been reached that are out of sight for our generation in Latin America. Per capita income, years of schooling, expenditure on health, printed pages read per person – all are beyond the healthy aspiration of 80 per cent of all Peruvians or Colombians, for example. But both here and there, political participation is low, power is limited and the mood bleak. For the United States Negro the signs pointing to integration and affluence have led all too often to a dead-end street.

During the last two years, the United States public has begun, very rapidly, to sympathize with the Negro sentiment against birth control in the ghetto. It is more shocking that the same public considers the poor overseas less sensitive and more gullible than those at home. More free advice in Brazil is supposed to turn the same trick that failed in the United States ghetto. A rebuff at home is to be taken seriously. That same rebuff overseas can be written off as folly and hysteria.

Last year in Brazil the Roman Catholic bishops and the communists combined to arouse public indignation against supposed favours extended by the military government to missionaries who import US-produced 'serpents' into Amazonia. The *serpentinas* (coils) were to be 'put into women' to render them sterile and to make Amazonia fit for colonization by Negroes imported from the United States, it was said.

The population expert bred around the North Atlantic easily interprets this as an outburst of sick imagination, rather than a symbolic protest against the United States serpent, soliciting tropical Eve to taste the apple of affluence. The economist, the planner and the doctor tacitly assume that all men are compulsive consumers and achievers yearning for well-paid jobs and wishing themselves in the shoes of those who have made it with fewer babies and more things. Such reasoning is based on a presumed 'law of human nature', but that presumption is at least as spurious as that preached by the Catholics. Too often missionaries condescendingly see their own idiosyncrasies as other people's natures.

Current American conversation in English about population unwittingly promotes an 'imperialist' bias. I suggest that we awaken to this bias and handle it as an acceptable variable in policy making. But equally I suggest that we beware of joining in the controversy over sin, usually conducted in Latin, or in the conspiracy to outbreed the paleface, which sounds Chinese. Only for a minority in Caracas or São Paulo could having a small family pay off immediately in higher living standards. For some 90 per cent, a meaningful improvement of such standards through birth control is beyond even their own temporal horizon. Most 'constructive' reasons peddled to this majority for family control, therefore, are deceptive. They usually imply a subtle indoctrination of 'middle-class values'. Acceptance of these values should forestall revolution against them. He who has learned to see wealth as the key sign of success, and children the major obstacle to growing rich, might now blame his children for his poverty. Few do, of course, because the argument is outrageous and also untrue.

To obtain the unreasoned assent of the majority all kinds of programmes are launched, most of them emphasizing immediate economic gain for the individual: direct rewards for each contraceptive treatment; oblique favours to small families; subtle, persuasive nudges connecting rising levels of expectation with low fertility. None works well enough. Why?

The fear of unattainable affluence does not intimidate the traditionally poor, just as the appeal to Hell has hardly influenced the sexual behaviour of devout Catholics. In any case, it is cynical to expect them to forego present enjoyment for the sake of a paradise that is open to others but is beyond, and will remain beyond, their reach. Nowhere do people breed according to White House policies or the Pope's commands. Socio-economic 'reasons' and moral codes are equally ineffective in introducing contraceptives. The use of ideology to push or oppose family planning is always a call to idolatry and, therefore, anti-human.

Ideology can arouse in some persons repressive forces and lead them to the use of contraceptives. Ideology can justify the desire for money, resentment, envy, unwillingness to share, the fear of risk or the desire to keep up with whatever Joneses. Ideology can explain these tendencies as contributions to political stability and productivity. But such reasoned sex control works only with a few, and they are strange and sick; their ideological motivations more frequently lead to irresponsible aggression than to discipline. Birth control is sold to the great majority under false pretences; for them, it is a blind alley to enrichment and there it does not decrease fertility. The use of ideology to motivate individual behaviour then is not only inhuman but it is also a fallacious policy. In such private matters, an appeal to patriotism, public spirit or religion is usually a good excuse – but rarely a good reason.

For example, let me compare the documented failure of teachers to turn out readers to the failure of welfare agencies to teach contraception. Teachers try to convince Juanito that he should want to read in order to be able to know, and work, and vote. But Juanito wants none of this, and there is no reason why he should. Reading will hardly lead to college unless he gets help from an uncle who is already there. And his vote in Latin America today is certainly less meaningful than ten years ago when the Alliance for Progress began. The one argument that might convince Juanito to stay in school is the need for a certificate that is supposed to open the door to a job – many years later.

People learn complex skills best if this process of learning affords the learner an opportunity to give clear shape to feelings of images that already exist in his heart. Only he who discovers the help of written words in order to face his fears and make them fade, and the power of words to seize his feelings and give them form, will want to dig deeper into other people's writing. The mere ability to decipher the written message will only lead indoctrinated masses to submit to instruction *by* schools and *for* factories, and at best enable them thereafter to use their leisure time to escape into cheap pulp-reading or make out the dubbed versions of foreign films.

Health workers tend to proceed very much like the teachers, except that they suggest that a pessary rather than a book will serve as the flying carpet into the better life. The product of the druggist, the stationer and the witch are used in the same style. Therefore, women who just swallow contraception are not better off than those who submit to print, or trust love potions or, superstitiously, Saint Anthony.

Schools succeed, at high cost, in producing literacy in a few children: only one out of four, in all of Latin America, go beyond the sixth grade. Welfare clinics have equally modest results in teaching adults contraception: only one out of four who seek advice ceases bearing children. Both agencies help to maintain the mould and the fold of the West. An economic comparison of school and clinic speaks for a shift of resources from literacy to birth control. On a short-term basis (let us say over fifteen years) the savings to a nation from one prevented life is much greater than the rise in productivity resulting from one schooled child.

Classroom and clinic both select better than they teach. If their combined budget were cut, it would probably not very significantly affect overall fertility. But such a cut in favour of other programmes cannot be taken into consideration unless it is understood to what degree the present school and health programmes are politically necessary.

Latin American society is regarded as barren even by some of its utopian dreamers. Even educational reformers speak and act as if teachers on this continent are unable to bring forth something truly new in education. Whenever effective adult education programmes are conceived and grow and threaten tradition, they are declared spurious and either aborted or ridiculed. Certainly large-scale programmes are never financed, the excuse being that on such a scale the methods proposed for them have never been proven.

Military governments must fear Socrates: he must be gaoled, exiled, ridiculed or driven underground. Few great, popular and respected Latin American teachers are employed in their own countries. If such men join the government, the Church or an international agency, they will be threatened by corruption through compromise.

There is a profound difference in the character of those who participate in Latin American educational structures, and this difference makes it difficult for North Americans to understand the reasons fundamental education is both more important and more dangerous in South America than it is in the ghetto. In Latin America the political establishment consists of the less than 3 per cent of heads of family who have graduated from secondary school. For this minority, any massive involvement of the unschooled in political argument threatens a profound change. Therefore programmes that might ultimately promote such involvement are either written off as self-defeating demagoguery, or quelled, quite understandably, as incitement to riot. Certainly they are not financed.

The prevailing uneven distribution of schooling is usually

considered a major obstacle to the spread of technological know-how and to effective political participation. Huge increases of school budgets for children are recommended as the one way of spreading political power and technological know-how, including contraception. This policy, in my opinion, rests on three erroneous assumptions: an overestimation of the educational efficiency of schools; an unrealistic expectation that a geometric increase of resources for schooling could ever become feasible; and a lack of confidence in the educational value of politically oriented education.

Paulo Freire, the exiled Brazilian educator, has shown that about 15 per cent of the illiterate adult population of any village can be taught to read and write in six weeks, and at a cost comparable to a fraction of one school year for a child. An additional 15 per cent can learn the same but more slowly. For that purpose he asks his team to prepare in each village a list of words that have the greatest intensity of meaning. Usually these words relate to politics and are, therefore, a focus of controversy. His literacy sessions are organized around the analysis of the chosen words. The persons attracted by this literacy programme are mostly those with political potential. We must assume that they are interested in dialogue and that learning to read and write its key words means for them a step to carry their political participation to new levels of intensity and effectiveness.

Obviously such education is selective. So are our present schools. The difference is that political potential makes the written page the place of encounter for the potentially subversive elements in society, rather than making it a sieve through which to pass those children who prove tolerant to compliance and qualified failure. Freire's alumni consume a diet that is different from the pulp and trash on which dropouts feed.

I will never forget an evening with Freire's pupils, hungry peasants in Sergipe, in early 1964. One man got up, struggled for words and finally put into one utterance the argument I want to make in this article: 'I could not sleep last night ... because last evening I wrote my name ... and I understood that I am I ... this means that *we* are responsible.'

Responsible citizenship and responsible parenthood go hand in hand. Both are the result of an experienced relatedness of the self to others. The discipline of spontaneous behaviour is effective, creative, and sustained only if it is accepted with other people in mind, The decision to act as responsible mate and parent implies participation in political life and acceptance of the discipline this demands. Today in Brazil this means readiness for revolutionary struggle.

In this perspective my suggestion to orient large-scale formal educational programmes for adults intensively towards family planning implies a commitment in favour of a political education. The struggle for political liberation and popular participation in Latin America can be rooted in new depth and awareness if it will spring from the recognition that, even in the most intimate domains of life, modern man must accept technology as a condition. Conducted in this style, education to modern parenthood could become a powerful form of agitation to help an uprooted mass grow into 'people'.

11 Planned Poverty: The End Result of Technical Assistance

At the beginning of the second development decade, at the time the 'Pearson Report' was presented to Robert McNamara it seemed important to discuss alternatives to the current notions of development, which, though based on supposedly irrefutable evidence, actually concealed highly questionable presuppositions.

It is now common to demand that the rich nations convert their war machine into a programme for the development of the Third World. The poorer four-fifths of humanity multiply unchecked while their per capita consumption actually declines. This population expansion and decrease of consumption threaten the industrialized nations, who may still, as a result, convert their defence budgets to the economic pacification of poor nations. And this in turn could produce irreversible despair, because the plough of the rich can do as much harm as their swords. United States trucks can do more lasting damage than United States tanks. It is easier to create mass demand for the former than for the latter. Only a minority needs heavy weapons, while a majority can become dependent on unrealistic levels of supply for such productive machines as modern trucks. Once the Third World has become a mass market for the goods, products, and processes which are designed by the rich for themselves, the discrepancy between demand for these Western artifacts and the supply will increase indefinitely. The family car cannot drive the poor into the jet age, nor can a school system provide the poor with education, nor can the family refrigerator ensure healthy food for them.

It is evident that only one man in a thousand in Latin America can afford a Cadillac, a heart operation or a Ph.D. This restriction on the goals of development does not make us despair of the fate of the Third World, and the reason is simple. We have not yet come to conceive of a Cadillac as necessary for good transportation, or of a heart operation as normal healthy care, or of a Ph.D. as the prerequisite of an acceptable education. In fact we recognize at once that the importation of Cadillacs should be heavily taxed in Peru, that an organ transplant clinic is a scandalous plaything to justify the concentration of more doctors in Bogotá, and that a betatron is beyond the teaching facilities of the University of São Paulo.

Unfortunately it is not held to be universally evident that the majority of Latin Americans – not only of our generation, but also of the next and the next again – cannot afford any kind of automobile, or any kind of hospitalization, or for that matter an elementary school education. We suppress our consciousness of this obvious reality because we hate to recognize the corner into which our imagination has been pushed. So persuasive is the power of the institutions we have created that they shape not only our preferences, but actually our sense of possibilities. We have forgotten how to speak about modern transportation that does not rely on automobiles and aeroplanes. Our conceptions of modern health care emphasize our ability to prolong the lives of the desperately ill. We have become unable to think of better education except in terms of more complex schools and of teachers trained for ever longer periods. Huge institutions producing costly services dominate the horizons of our inventiveness.

We have embodied our world view into our institutions and are now their prisoners. Factories, news media, hospitals, governments and schools produce goods and services packaged to contain our view of the world. We – the rich – conceive of progress as the expansion of these establishments. We conceive of heightened mobility as luxury and safety packaged by General Motors or Boeing. We conceive of improving the general well-being as increasing the supply of doctors and hospitals, which package health along with protracted suffering. We have come to identify our need for further learning with the demand for ever longer confinement to classrooms. In other words, we have packaged education with custodial care, certification for jobs and the right to vote, and wrapped them all together with indoctrination in the Christian, liberal or communist virtues.

In less than a hundred years industrial society has moulded patent solutions to basic human needs and converted us to the belief that man's needs were shaped by the Creator as demands for the products we have invented. This is as true for Russia and Japan as for the North Atlantic community. The consumer is trained for obsolescence, which means continuing loyalty toward the same producers who will give him the same basic packages in different quality or new wrappings.

Industrialized societies can provide such packages for personal consumption for most of their citizens, but this is no proof that these societies are sane, or economical, or that they promote life. The contrary is true. The more the citizen is trained in the consumption of packaged goods and services, the less effective he seems to become in shaping his environment. His energies and finances are consumed in procuring ever new models of his staples, and the environment becomes a by-product of his own consumption habits.

The design of the 'package deals' of which I speak is the main cause of the high cost of satisfying basic needs. So long as every man 'needs' his car, our cities must endure longer traffic jams and absurdly expensive remedies to relieve them. So long as health means maximum length of survival, our sick will get ever more extraordinary surgical interventions and the drugs required to deaden their consequent pain. So long as we want to use school to get children out of their parents' hair or to keep them off the street and out of the labour force, our young will be retained in endless schooling and will need ever increasing incentives to endure the ordeal.

Rich nations now benevolently impose a strait jacket of traffic jams, hospital confinements and classrooms on the poor nations, and by international agreement call this 'development'. The rich and schooled and old of the world try to share their dubious blessings by foisting their prepackaged solutions on to the Third World. Traffic jams develop in São Paulo while almost a million North-Eastern Brazilians flee the drought by walking five hundred miles. Latin American doctors get trained at The Hospital for Special Surgery in New York, which they apply to only a few, while amoebic dysentery remains endemic in slums where 90 per cent of the population live. A tiny minority gets advanced education in basic science in North America – not infrequently paid for by their own governments. If they return at all to Bolivia, they become second-rate teachers of pretentious subjects at La Paz or Cochabamba. The rich export outdated versions of their standard models.

The Alliance for Progress is a good example of benevolent production for underdevelopment. Contrary to its slogans, it did succeed – as an alliance for the progress of the consuming classes, and for the domestication of the Latin American masses. The Alliance has been a major step in modernizing the consumption patterns of the middle classes in South America by integrating them with the dominant culture of the North American metropolis. At the same time, the Alliance has modernized the aspirations of the majority of citizens and fixed their demands on unavailable products.

Each car which Brazil puts on the road denies fifty people good transportation by bus. Each merchandised refrigerator reduces the chance of building a community freezer. Every dollar spent in Latin America on doctors and hospitals costs a hundred lives, to adopt a phrase of Jorge de Ahumada, the brilliant Chilean economist. Had each dollar been spent on providing safe drinking water, a hundred lives could have been saved. Each dollar spent on schooling means more privileges for the few at the cost of the many; at best it increases the number of those who before dropping out, have been taught that those who stay longer have earned the right to more power, wealth and prestige. What such schooling does is to teach the schooled the superiority of the better schooled.

All Latin American countries are frantically intent on expanding their school systems. No country now spends less than the equivalent of 18 per cent of tax-derived public income on education – which means schooling – and many countries spend almost double that. But even with these huge investments, no country yet succeeds in giving five full years of education to more than one-third of its population; supply and demand for schooling grow geometrically apart. And what is true about schooling is equally true about the products of most institutions in the process of modernization in the Third World.

Continued technological refinements of products which are already established on the market frequently benefit the producer far more than the consumer. The more complex production processes tend to enable only the largest producer to replace outmoded models continually, and to focus the demand of the consumer on the marginal improvement of what he buys, no matter what the concomitant side effects: higher prices, diminished life span, less general usefulness, higher cost of repairs. Think of the multiple uses for a simple tin opener, whereas an electric one, if it works at all, opens only some kinds of tins, and costs one hundred times as much.

This is equally true for a piece of agricultural machinery and for an academic degree. The Mid-Western farmer can become convinced of his need for a four-axle vehicle which can go 70 m.p.h. on the highways, has an electric windscreen wiper and upholstered seats, and can be turned in for a new one within a year or two. Most of the world's farmers don't need such speed, nor have they ever met with such comfort, nor are they interested in obsolescence. They need low-priced transport, in a world where time is not money, where manual wipers suffice, and where a piece of heavy equipment should outlast a generation. Such a mechanical donkey requires entirely different engineering and design than one produced for the United States market. This vehicle is not in production.

Most of South America needs paramedical workers who can function for indefinite periods without the supervision of a qualified doctor. Instead of establishing a process to train mid-wives and visiting healers who know how to use a very limited arsenal of medicines while working independently, Latin American universities establish every year a new school of specialized nursing or nursing administration to prepare professionals who can function only in a hospital, and pharmacists who know how to sell increasingly more dangerous drugs.

The world is reaching an impasse where two processes converge: ever more men have fewer basic choices. The increase in population is widely publicized and creates panic. The decrease in fundamental choice causes anguish and is consistently overlooked. The population explosion overwhelms the imagination, but the progressive atrophy of social imagination is rationalized as an increase of choise between brands. The two processes converge in a dead end: the population explosion provides more consumers for everything from food to contraceptives, while our shrinking imagination can conceive of no other ways of satisfying their demands except through the packages now on sale in the admired societies.

I will focus successively on these two factors, since, in my opinion, they form the two coordinates which together permit us to define underdevelopment.

In most Third World countries, the population grows, and so does the middle class. Income, consumption and the well-being of the middle class are all growing while the gap between this class and the mass of people widens. Even where per capita consumption is rising, the majority of men have less food now than in 1945, less actual care in sickness, less meaningful work, less protection. This is partly a consequence of polarized consumption and partly caused by the breakdown of traditional family and culture. More people suffer from hunger, pain and exposure in 1969 than they did at the end of the Second World War, not only numerically, but also as a percentage of the world population.

These concrete consequences of underdevelopment are rampant; but underdevelopment is also a state of mind, and understanding it as a state of mind, or as a form of consciousness, is the critical problem. Underdevelopment as a state of mind occurs when mass needs are converted to the demand for new brands of packaged solutions which are forever beyond the reach of the majority. Underdevelopment in this sense is rising rapidly even in countries where the supply of classrooms, calories, cars and clinics is also rising. The ruling groups in these countries build up services which have been designed for an affluent culture; once they have monopolized demand in this way, they can never satisfy majority needs.

Underdevelopment as a form of consciousness is an extreme result of what we can call in the language of both Marx and Freud *Verdinglichung*, or reification. By reification I mean the hardening of the perception of real needs into the demand for mass manufactured products. I mean the translation of thirst into the need for a Coke. This kind of reification occurs in the manipulation of primary human needs by vast bureaucratic organizations which have succeeded in dominating the imagination of potential consumers.

Let me return to my example taken from the field of education. The intense promotion of schooling leads to so close an identification of school attendance and education that in everyday language the two terms are interchangeable. Once the imagination of an entire population has been 'schooled', or indoctrinated to believe that school has a monopoly on formal education, then the illiterate can be taxed to provide free high-school and university education for the children of the rich.

Underdevelopment is the result of rising levels of aspiration achieved through the intensive marketing of 'patent' products. In this sense, the dynamic underdevelopment that is now taking place is the exact opposite of what I believe education to be: namely, the awakening awareness of new levels of human potential and the use of one's creative powers to foster human life. Underdevelopment, however, implies the surrender of social consciousness to prepackaged solutions.

The process by which the marketing of 'foreign' products increases underdevelopment is frequently understood in the most superficial ways. The same man who feels indignation at the sight of a Coca-Cola plant in a Latin American slum often feels pride at the sight of a new normal school growing up alongside. He resents the evidence of a foreign 'licence' attached to a soft drink which he would like to see replaced by 'Cola-Mex'. But the same man is willing to impose schooling – at all costs – on his fellow citizens, and is unaware of the invisible licence by which this institution is deeply enmeshed in the world market.

Some years ago I watched workmen putting up a sixty-foot Coca-Cola sign on a desert plain in the Mexquital. A serious drought and famine had just swept over the Mexican highland. My host, a poor Indian in Ixmiquilpan, had just offered his visitors a tiny tequila glass of the costly black sugar-water. When I recall this scene I still feel anger; but I feel much more incensed when I remember UNESCO meetings at which well-meaning and well-paid bureaucrats seriously discussed Latin American school curricula, and when I think of the speeches of enthusiastic liberals advocating the need for more schools.

The fraud perpetrated by the salesmen of schools is less obvious but much more fundamental than the self-satisfied salesmanship of the Coca-Cola or Ford representative, because the schoolman hooks his people on a much more demanding drug. Elementary school attendance is not a harmless luxury, but more like the coca chewing of the Andean Indian, which harnesses the worker to the boss.

The higher the dose of schooling an individual has received, the more depressing his experience of withdrawal. The seventh-grade dropout feels his inferiority much more acutely than the dropout from the third grade. The schools of the Third World administer their opium with much more effect than the Churches of other epochs. As the mind of a society is progressively schooled, step by step its individuals lose their sense that it might be possible to live without being inferior to others. As the majority shifts from the land into the city, the hereditary inferiority of the peon is replaced by the inferiority of the school dropout who is held personally responsible for his failure. Schools rationalize the divine origin of social stratification with much more rigour than churches have ever done.

Until this day no Latin American country has declared youthful underconsumers of Coca-Cola or cars as lawbreakers, while all Latin American countries have passed laws which define the early dropout as a citizen who has not fulfilled his legal obligations. The Brazilian government recently almost doubled the number of years during which schooling is legally compulsory and free. From now on any Brazilian dropout under the age of sixteen will be faced during his lifetime with the reproach that he did not take advantage of a legally obligatory privilege. This law was passed in a country where not even the most optimistic could foresee the day when such levels of schooling would be provided for only 25 per cent of the young. The adoption of international standards of schooling forever condemns most Latin Americans to marginality or exclusion from social life – in a word, underdevelopment.

The translation of social goals into levels of consumption is not limited to only a few countries. Across all frontiers of culture, ideology and geography today, nations are moving towards the establishment of their own car factories, their own medical and normal schools – and most of these are, at best, poor imitations of foreign and largely North American models.

The Third World is in need of a profound revolution of its institutions. The revolutions of the last generation were overwhelmingly political. A new group of men with a new set of ideological justifications assumed power to administer fundamentally the same scholastic, medical and market institutions in the interest of a new group of clients. Since the institutions have not radically changed, the new group of clients remains approximately the same size as that previously served. This appears clearly in the case of education. Per pupil costs of schooling are today comparable everywhere since the standards used to evaluate the quality of schooling tend to be internationally shared. Access to publicly financed education, considered as access to school, everywhere depends on per capita income. (Places like

China and North Vietnam might be meaningful exceptions.)

Everywhere in the Third World modern institutions are grossly unproductive, with respect to the egalitarian purposes for which they are being reproduced. But so long as the social imagination of the majority has not been destroyed by its fixation on these institutions, there is more hope of planning an institutional revolution in the Third World than among the rich. Hence the urgency of the task of developing workable alternatives to 'modern' solutions.

Underdevelopment is at the point of becoming chronic in many countries. The revolution of which I speak must begin to take place before this happens. Education again offers a good example: chronic educational underdevelopment occurs when the demand for schooling becomes so widespread that the total concentration of educational resources on the school system becomes a unanimous political demand. At this point the separation of education from schooling becomes impossible.

The only feasible answer to ever increasing underdevelopment is a response to basic needs that is planned as a long-range goal for areas which will always have a different capital structure. It is easier to speak about alternatives to existing institutions, services and products than to define them with precision. It is not my purpose either to paint a Utopia or to engage in scripting scenarios for an alternative future. We must be satisfied with examples indicating simple directions that research should take.

Some such examples have already been given. Buses are alternatives to a multitude of private cars. Vehicles designed for slow transportation on rough terrain are alternatives to standard lorries. Safe water is an alternative to high-priced surgery. Medical workers are an alternative to doctors and nurses. Community food storage is an alternative to expensive kitchen equipment. Other alternatives could be discussed by the dozen. Why not, for example, consider walking as a long-range alternative for locomotion by machine, and explore the demands which this would impose on the city planner? And why can't the building of shelters be standardized, elements be precast, and each citizen be obliged to learn in a year of public service how to construct his own sanitary housing?

It is harder to speak about alternatives in education, partly because schools have recently so completely preempted the available educational resources of good will, imagination and money. But even here we can indicate the direction in which research must be conducted.

At present, schooling is conceived as graded, curricular, class attendance by children, for about one thousand hours yearly during an uninterrupted succession of years. On the average, Latin American countries can provide each citizen with between eight and thirty months of this service. Why not, instead, make one or two months a year obligatory for all citizens below the age of thirty?

Money is now spent largely on children, but an adult can be taught to read in one-tenth the time and for one-tenth the cost it takes to teach a child. In the case of the adult there is an immediate return on the investment, whether the main importance of his learning is seen in his new insight, political awareness and willingness to assume responsibility for his family's size and future, or whether the emphasis is placed on increased productivity. There is a double return in the case of the adult, because not only can he contribute to the education of his children, but to that of other adults as well. In spite of these advantages, basic literacy programmes have little or no support in Latin America, where schools have a first call on all public resources. Worse, these programmes are actually ruthlessly suppressed in Brazil and elsewhere, where military support of the feudal or industrial oligarchy has thrown off its former benevolent disguise.

Another possibility is harder to define, because there is as yet no example to point to. We must therefore imagine the use of public resources for education distributed in such a way as to give every citizen a minimum chance. Education will become a political concern of the majority of voters only when each individual has a precise sense of the educational resources that are owing to him – and some idea of how to sue for them. Something like a universal G.I. Bill of Rights could be imagined, dividing the public resources assigned to education by the number of children who are legally of school age, and making sure that a child who did not take advantage of his credit at the age of seven, eight or nine would have the accumulated benefits at his disposal at age ten.

What would the pitiful education credit which a Latin

American republic could offer to its children provide? Almost all of the basic supply of books, pictures, blocks, games and toys that are totally absent from the homes of the really poor, but enable a middle-class child to learn the alphabet, the colours, shapes and other classes of objects and experiences which ensure his educational progress. The choice between these things and schools is obvious. Unfortuntately, the poor, for whom alone the choice is real, never get to exercise this choice.

Defining alternatives to the products and institutions which now preempt the field is difficult, not only, as I have been trying to show, because these products and institutions shape our conception of reality itself, but also because the construction of new possibilities requires a concentration of will and intelligence in a higher degree than ordinarily occurs by chance. This concentration of will and intelligence on the solution of particular problems regardless of their nature we have become accustomed over the last century to call research.

I must make clear, however, what kind of research I am talking about. I am not talking about basic research either in physics, engineering, genetics, medicine or learning. The work of such men as F. H. C. Crick, Jean Piaget and Murray Gell-Mann must continue to enlarge our horizons in other fields of science. The labs and libraries and specially trained collaborators these men need cause them to congregate in the few research capitals of the world. Their research can provide the basis for new work on practically any product.

I am not speaking here of the billions of dollars annually spent on applied research, for this money is largely spent by existing institutions on the perfection and marketing of their own products. Applied research is money spent on making planes faster and airports safer; on making medicines more specific and powerful and doctors capable of handling their deadly side effects; on packaging more learning into classrooms; on methods to administer large bureaucracies. This is the kind of research for which some kind of counterfoil must somehow be developed if we are to have any chance to come up with basic alternatives to the automobile, the hospital, and the school, and any of the many other so-called 'evidently necessary implements for modern life'.

C.A. – 8

I have in mind a different, and peculiarly difficult, kind of research, which has been largely neglected up to now, for obvious reasons. I am calling for research on alternatives to the products which now dominate the market; to hospitals and the profession dedicated to keeping the sick alive; to schools and the packaging process which refuses education to those who are not of the right age, who have not gone through the right curriculum, who have not sat in a classroom a sufficient number of successive hours, who will not pay for their learning with submission to custodial care, screening and certification or with indoctrination in the values of the dominant elite.

This counter-research on fundamental alternatives to current prepackaged solutions is the element most critically needed if the poor nations are to have a liveable future. Such counter-research is distinct from most of the work done in the name of the 'year 2000', because most of that work seeks radical changes in social patterns through adjustments in the organization of an already advanced technology. The counter-research of which I speak must take as one of its assumptions the continued lack of capital in the Third World.

The difficulties of such research are obvious. The researcher must first of all doubt what is obvious to every eye. Second, he must persuade those who have the power of decision to act against their own short-run interests or bring pressure on them to do so. And, finally, he must survive as an individual in a world he is attempting to change fundamentally so that his fellows among the privileged minority see him as a destroyer of the very ground on which all of us stand. He knows that if he should succeed in the interest of the poor, technologically advanced societies still might envy the 'poor' who adopt this vision.

There is a normal course for those who make development policies, whether they live in North or South America, in Russia or Israel. It is to define development and to set its goals in ways with which they are familiar, which they are accustomed to use in order to satisfy their own needs, and which permit them to work through the institutions over which they have power or control. This formula has failed, and must fail. There is not enough money in the world for development to succeed along these lines, not even in the combined arms and space budgets of the superpowers.

An analogous course is followed by those who are trying to make political revolutions, especially in the Third World. Usually they promise to make the familiar privileges of the present elites, such as schooling, hospital care, etc., accessible to all citizens; and they base this vain promise on the belief that a change in political regime will permit them to sufficiently enlarge the institutions which produce these privileges. The promise and appeal of the revolutionary are therefore just as threatened by the counter-research I propose as is the market of the now dominant producers.

In Vietnam a people on bicycles and armed with sharpened bamboo sticks have brought to a standstill the most advanced machinery for research and production ever devised. We must seek survival in a Third World in which human ingenuity can peacefully outwit machined might. The only way to reverse the disastrous trend to increasing underdevelopment, hard as it is, is to learn to laugh at accepted solutions in order to change the demands which make them necessary. Only free men can change their minds and be surprised; and while no men are completely free, some are freer than others.

12 A Constitution for Cultural Revolution

At the invitation of the publishers of the annual *Great Ideas* volume I wrote the article which follows, and which I feel is an appropriate conclusion to this book. Its purpose was to initiate discussion about the need of constitutional principles which would guarantee an ongoing cultural revolution in a technological society. The article originally appeared in *Great Ideas Today* 1970, published by Encyclopaedia Britannica, Inc.

During the decade just past we have got used to seeing the world divided into two parts: the developed and the underdeveloped. People in the development business may prefer to speak of the developed nations and the less developed or developing nations. This terminology suggests that development is both good and inevitable. Others, especially protagonists of revolutionary change, speak of the 'Third World' and wait for the day when the wretched of the earth will rise in armed revolt against the imperialist powers and shift control over existing institutions from North to South, from White to Black, from metropolis to colony.

A vulgar example of the first assumption is the Rockefeller Report on the Americas. Its doctrine is aptly summed up by President Nixon: 'This I pledge to you tonight: the nation that went to the moon in peace for all mankind is ready to share its technology in peace with its nearest neighbours.' The governor, in turn, proposes that keeping the pledge might require a lot of additional weaponry in South America.

The Pearson Report on partnership in development is a much more sophisticated example of the development mentality. It outlines policies which will permit a few more countries to join the charmed circle of the consumer nations but which will actually increase the poverty of the poor half in these same countries: because the strategies proposed will sell them ever more thoroughly on goods and services ever more expensive and out of their reach. The policy goals of most revolutionary movements and governments I know – and I do not know Mao's China – reflect another type of cynicism. Their leaders make futile promises that – once in power for a sufficient length of time – more of everything which the masses have learned to know and to envy as privileges of the rich will be produced and distributed. Both the purveyors of development and the preachers of revolution advocate more of the same. They define more education as more schooling, better health as more doctors, higher mobility as more high-speed vehicles. The salesmen for United States industry, the experts for the World Bank and ideologues of power for the poor seem to forget that heart surgery and college degrees remain beyond the reach of the majority for generations.

The goals of development are always and everywhere stated in terms of consumer value packages standardized around the North Atlantic – and therefore always and everywhere imply more privileges for a few. Political reorganization cannot change this fact; it can only rationalize it. Different ideologies create different minorities of privileged consumers, but heart surgery or a university education is always priced out of range for all but a few: be they the rich, the orthodox or the most fascinating subjects for experiments by surgeons or pedagogues.

Underdevelopment is the result of a state of mind common to both socialist and capitalist countries. Present development goals are neither desirable nor reasonable. Unfortunately anti-imperialism is no antidote. Although exploitation of poor countries is an undeniable reality, current nationalism is merely the affirmation of the right of colonial elites to repeat history and follow the road travelled by the rich towards the universal consumption of internationally marketed packages, a road which can ultimately lead only to universal pollution and universal frustration.

The central issue of our time remains the fact that the rich are getting richer and the poor, poorer. This hard fact is often obscured by another apparently contradictory fact. In the rich countries the poor expect a quantity and quality of commodities beyond the dreams of Louis XIV, while many of the so-called developing countries enjoy much higher economic growth rates than those of industralized countries at a similar stage of their own histories. From icebox to toilet and from antibiotic to television, conveniences are found necessary in Harlem which Washington could not have imagined at Mount Vernon, just as Bolívar could not have foreseen the social polarization now inevitable in Caracas. But neither rising levels of minimum consumption in the rich countries nor of urban consumption in the poor countries can close the gap between rich and poor nations or between the rich and poor of any one nation. Modern poverty is a by-product of a world market catering to the ideologies of an industrial middle class. Modern poverty is built into an international community where demand is engineered through publicity to stimulate the production of standard commodities. In such a market, expectations are standardized and must always outrace marketable resources.

In the United States, for all its gargantuan prosperity, real poverty levels rise faster than the median income. In the capital-starved countries, median incomes move rapidly away from rising averages. Most goods now produced for rich and poor alike in the United States are beyond the reach of all but a few in other areas. In both rich and poor nations consumption is polarized while expectation is equalized.

During the decade now beginning we must learn a new language, a language that speaks not of development and under-development but of true and false ideas about man, his needs and his potential. Development programmes all over the world progressively lead to violence, either in the form of repression or of rebellion. This is neither due to the evil intentions of capitalists nor to the ideological rigidity of communists, but to the radical inability of men to tolerate the by-products of industrial and welfare institutions developed in the early industrial age. In the late 1960s attention has suddenly been drawn to the inability of man to survive his industry. During the late 1960s it has become evident that less than 10 per cent of the human race consumes more than 50 per cent of the world's resources, and produces 90 per cent of the physical pollution which threatens to extinguish the biosphere. But this is only one aspect of the paradox of present development. During the early 1970s it will become equally clear that welfare institutions have an analogous regressive effect. The international institutionalization of social service, medicine and education which is generally identified with development has equally overwhelming destructive by-products.

We need an alternative programme, an alternative both to development and to merely political revolution. Let me call this alternative programme either institutional or cultural revolution, because its aim is the transformation of both public and personal reality. The political revolutionary wants to improve existing institutions – their productivity and the quality and distribution of their products. His vision of what is desirable and possible is based on consumption habits developed during the last hundred years. The cultural revolutionary believes that these habits have radically distorted our view of what human beings can have and want. He questions the reality that others take for granted, a reality that, in his view, is the artificial by-product of contemporary institutions, created and reinforced by them in pursuit of their short-term ends. The political revolutionary concentrates on schooling and tooling for the environment that the rich countries, socialist or capitalist, have engineered. The cultural revolutionary risks the future on the educability of man.

The cultural revolutionary must not only be distinguished from the political magician but also from both the neo-Luddite and the promoter of intermediary technology. The former behaves as if the noble savage could either be restored to the throne or the Third World transformed into a reservation for him. He opposes the internal combustion engine rather than opposing its packaging into a product designed for exclusive use by the man who owns it. Thus the Luddite blames the producer; the institutional revolutionary tries to reshape the design and distribution of the product. The Luddite blames the machine; the cultural revolutionary heightens awareness that it produces needless demands. The cultural revolutionary must also be distinguished from the promoter of intermediary technology who is frequently merely a superior tactician paving the road to totally manipulated consumption.

Let me illustrate what I mean by a cultural revolution within one major international institution, by taking as an example the institution which currently produces education. I mean, of course, obligatory schooling: full-time attendance of age-specific groups at a graded curriculum.

Latin America has decided to school itself into development. This decision results in the production of homemade inferiority. With every school that is built, another seed of institutional corruption is planted, and this is in the name of growth.

Schools affect individuals and characterize nations. Individuals merely get a bad deal; nations are irreversibly degraded when they build schools to help their citizens play at international competition. For the individual, school is always a gamble. The chances may be very slim, but everyone shoots for the same jackpot. Of course, as any professional gambler knows, it is the rich who win in the end and the poor who get hooked. And if the poor man manages to stay in the game for a while, he will feel the pain even more sharply when he does lose, as he almost inevitably must. Primary-school dropouts in a Latin American city find it increasingly difficult to get industrial jobs.

But no matter how high the odds, everyone plays the game, for after all, there is only one game in town. A scholarship may be a long shot, but it is a chance to become equal to the world's best-trained bureaucrats. And the student who fails can console himself with the knowledge that the cards were stacked against him from the outset.

More and more, men begin to believe that, in the schooling game, the loser gets only what he deserves. The belief in the ability of schools to label people correctly is already so strong that people accept their vocational and marital fate with a gambler's resignation. In cities, this faith in school-slotting is on the way to sprouting a more creditable meritocracy – a state of mind in which each citizen believes that he deserves the place assigned to him by school. A perfect meritocracy, in which there would be no excuses, is not yet upon us, and I believe it can be avoided. It must be avoided, since a perfect meritocracy would not only be hellish, it would be hell.

Educators appeal to the gambling instinct of the entire population when they raise money for schools. They advertise the jackpot without mentioning the odds. And those odds are high indeed for someone who is born brown, poor or in the pampa. In Latin America, no country is prouder of its legally obligatory admission-free school system than Argentina. Yet only one Argentinian of five thousand born into the lower half of the population gets as far as the university.

What is only a wheel of fortune for an individual is a spinning wheel of irreversible underdevelopment for a nation. The high cost of schooling turns education into a scarce resource, as poor countries accept that a certain number of years in school makes an educated man. More money gets spent on fewer people. In poor countries, the school pyramid of the rich countries takes on the shape of an obelisk, or a rocket. School inevitably gives individuals who attend it and then drop out, as well as those who don't make it at all, a rationale for their own inferiority. But for poor nations, obligatory schooling is a monument to self-inflicted inferiority. To buy the schooling hoax is to purchase a ticket for the back seat in a bus headed nowhere.

Schooling encrusts the poorest nations at the bottom of the

educational bucket. The school systems of Latin America are fossilized deposits of a dream begun a century ago. The school pyramid is a-building from top to bottom throughout Latin America. All countries spend more than 20 per cent of their national budget and nearly 5 per cent of their gross national product on its construction. Teachers constitute the largest profession and their children are frequently the largest group of students in the upper grades. Fundamental education is either redefined as the foundation for schooling, and therefore placed beyond the reach of the unschooled and the early dropout, or is defined as a remedy for the unschooled, which will only frustrate him into accepting inferiority. Even the poorest countries continue to spend disproportionate sums on graduate schools – gardens which ornament the penthouses of skyscrapers built in a slum.

Bolivia is well on the way to suicide by an overdose of schooling. This impoverished, landlocked country creates papiermâché bridges to prosperity by spending more than a third of its entire budget on public education and half as much again on private schools. A full half of this educational misspending is consumed by 1 per cent of the school-age population. In Bolivia, the university student's share of public funds is a thousand times greater than that of his fellow citizen of median income. Most Bolivian people live outside the city, yet only 2 per cent of the rural population makes it to the fifth grade. This discrimination was legally sanctioned in 1967 by declaring grade school obligatory for all – a law that made most people criminal by fiat and the rest immoral exploiters by decree. In 1970, the university entrance examinations were abolished with a flourish of egalitarian rhetoric. At first glance, it does seem a libertarian advance to legislate that all high school graduates have a right to enter the university – until you realize that less than 2 per cent of Bolivians finish high school.

Bolivia may be an extreme example of schooling in Latin America. But on an international scale, Bolivia *is* typical. Few African or Asian countries have attained the progress now taken for granted there.

Cuba is perhaps an example of the other extreme. Fidel Castro has tried to create a major cultural revolution. He has reshaped the academic pyramid, and promised that by 1980 the universities can be closed, since all of Cuba will be one big university with higher learning going on at work and leisure. Yet the Cuban pyramid is still a pyramid. There is no doubt that the redistribution of privilege, the redefinition of social goals and the popular participation in the achievement of these goals have reached spectacular heights in Cuba since the revolution. For the moment, however, Cuba is showing only that, under exceptional political conditions, the base of the present school system can be expanded exceptionally. But there are built-in limits to the elasticity of present institutions, and Cuba is at the point of reaching them. The Cuban revolution will work – within these limits. Which means only that Dr Castro will have masterminded a faster road to a bourgeois meritocracy than those previously taken by capitalists or bolsheviks. Sometimes, when he is not promising schools for all, Fidel hints at a policy of deschooling for all, and the Isle of Pines seems to be a laboratory for redistribution of educational functions to other social institutions. But unless Cuban educators admit that work-education which is effective in a rural economy can be even more effective in an urban one, Cuba's institutional revolution will not begin. No cultural revolution can be built on the denial of reality.

As long as communist Cuba continues to promise obligatory high-school completion by the end of this decade, it is, in this regard, institutionally no more promising than fascist Brazil, which has made a similar promise. In both Brazil and Cuba, enough girls have already been born to double the number of potential mothers in the 1980s. Per capita resources available for education can hardly be expected to double in either country, and even if they could, no progress would have been made at all. In development-mad Brazil and in humanist Cuba, waiting for Godot is equally futile. Without a radical change in their institutional goals, both 'revolutions' must make fools of themselves. Unfortunately, both seem headed for manifest foolishness, albeit by different routes. The Cubans allow work, party and community involvement to nibble away at the school year, and call this radical education, while the Brazilians let United States experts peddle teaching devices that only raise the per capita cost of classroom attendance.

The production of inferiority through schooling is more evident in poor countries and perhaps more painful in rich countries. The 10 per cent in the United States with the highest incomes can provide most of the education for their children through private institutions. Yet they also succeed in obtaining ten times more of the public resources devoted to education than the poorest 10 per cent if the population. In Soviet Russia a more puritanical belief in meritocracy makes the concentration of schooling privileges on the children of urban professionals even more painful.

In the shadow of each national school-pyramid, an international caste system is wedded to an international class structure. Countries are ranged like castes, whose educational dignity is determined by the average years of schooling of its citizens. Individual citizens of all countries achieve a symbolic mobility through a class system which makes each man accept the place he believes to have merited.

The political revolutionary strengthens the demand for schooling by futilely promising that under his administration more learning and increased earning will become available to all through more schooling. He contributes to the modernization of a world class structure and a modernization of poverty. It remains the task of the cultural revolutionary to overcome the delusions on which the support of school is based and to outline policies for the radical deschooling of society.

The basic reason for all this is that schooling comes in quanta. Less than so much is no good and the minimum quantum carries a minimum price. It is obvious that with schools of equal quality a poor child can never catch up with a rich one, nor a poor country with a rich country. It is equally obvious that poor children and poor countries never have equal schools but always poorer ones, and thus fall ever further behind, so long as they depend on schools for their education.

Another illusion is that most learning is a result of teaching. Teaching may contribute to certain kinds of learning under certain circumstances. The strongest motivated student faced with the task of learning a new code may benefit greatly from the discipline we now associate mostly with the old-fashioned schoolmaster. But most people acquire most of their insight, knowledge and skill outside school – and in school only in so far as school in a few rich countries becomes their place of confinement during an increasing part of their lives. The radical deschooling of society begins, therefore, with the unmasking by cultural revolutionaries of the myth of schooling. It continues with the struggle to liberate other men's minds from the false ideology of schooling – an ideology which makes domestication by schooling inevitable. In its final and positive stage it is the struggle for the right to educational freedom.

A cultural revolutionary must fight for legal protection from the imposition of any obligatory graded curriculum. The first article of a bill of rights for a modern and humanist society corresponds to the first amendment of the United States Constitution. The state shall make no law with respect to an establishment of education. There shall be no graded curriculum, obligatory for all. To make this disestablishment effective, we need a law forbidding discrimination in hiring, voting or admission to centres of learning based on previous attendance at some curriculum. This guarantee would not exclude specific tests of competence, but would remove the present absurd discrimination in favour of the person who learns a given skill with the largest expenditure of public funds. A third legal reform would guarantee the right of each citizen to an equal share of public educational resources, the right to verify his share of these resources, and the right to sue for them if they are denied. A generalized G.I. bill, or an edu-credit card in the hand of every citizen, would effectively implement this third guarantee.

Abolition of obligatory schooling, abolition of job discrimination in favour of persons who have acquired their learning at a higher cost, plus establishment of edu-credit, would permit the development of a free exchange for educational services. According to present political ideology, this exchange could be influenced by various devices: premiums paid to those who acquire certain needed skills, interest-bearing edu-credit to increase the privileges of those who use it later in life, advantages for industries that incorporate additional formal training into the work routine.

A fourth guarantee to protect the consumer against the monopoly of the educational market would be analogous to anti-trust laws.

I have shown in the case of education that a cultural or institutional revolution depends upon the clarification of reality. Development as now conceived is just the contrary: management of the environment and the tooling of man to fit into it. Cultural revolution is a review of the reality of man and a redefinition of the world in terms which support this reality. Development is the attempt to create an environment and then educate at great cost to pay for it.

A bill of rights for modern man cannot produce cultural revolution. It is merely a manifesto. I have outlined the principles of an educational bill of rights. These principles can be generalized.

The disestablishment of schooling can be generalized to freedom from monopoly in the satisfaction of any basic need. Discrimination on the basis of prior schooling can be generalized to discrimination in any institution because of underconsumption or underprivilege in another. A guarantee of equal education resources is a guarantee against regressive taxation. An educational anti-trust law is obviously merely a special case of anti-trust laws in general, which in turn are statutory implementations of constitutional guarantees against monopoly.

The social and psychological destruction inherent in obligatory schooling is merely an illustration of the destruction implicit in all international institutions which now dictate the kinds of goods, services, and welfare available to satisfy basic human needs. Only a cultural and institutional revolution which re-establishes man's control over his environment can arrest the violence by which development of institutions is now imposed by a few for their own interest. Maybe Marx has said it better, criticising Ricardo and his school: 'They want production to be limited to "useful things", but they forget that the production of too many *useful* things results in too many *useless* people.'

Deschooling Society

Ivan D. Illich

Is schooling the same thing as education? Obviously not. We all learn day by day, and most of us, to be honest, can find little in our lives which schooling has directly and profoundly influenced. Two questions emerge. What is it then that has given schooling such enormous and widespread prestige in all societies throughout the world? And what is it that schooling actually does if its educational function is in doubt?

Ivan Illich argues in this eloquent and persuasive book that school has the prestige it does because it is one of the major means by which the status quo is preserved. It is not only inefficient in terms of education, but also profoundly divisive. *Deschooling Society* has already become a classic statement of a new and disturbing view of the school as an institution. It is amply possible to disagree with Illich; it is hardly possible to ignore him.

'His assault on the school . . . demands to be considered seriously'
Peter Jenkins, *Guardian*

'*Deschooling Society* is one of the most genuine subversive books in that it amounts to a radical re-interpretation of social reality'
David Gow, *Scotsman*

School is Dead

Everett Reimer

Most of the children in the world are not in school. Most of those who are drop out as soon as possible. Most countries in the world can only afford to give their children the barest minimum of education, while the costs of schooling are everywhere rising faster than enrolments, and faster than national income. Schools are for most people what the author calls 'institutional props for privilege', and yet at the same time they are the major instruments of social mobility. But at what cost in terms of true learning, true creativity, true democracy? And at what ultimate cost to the societies which perpetuate themselves in this way?

This is the background to Everett Reimer's important, wide-ranging and intelligent book. The most urgent priority, he argues, is for a consideration of *alternatives* in education – alternative content, organization and finance. Above all, we urgently need alternative views of education itself, its nature and possible functions in the society of the future.

'Illich and Reimer have asked some of the profoundest questions about education today'
Ian Lister, *The Times Higher Education Supplement*

'The case against universal compulsory schooling is a substantial one and Everett Reimer thumps it out in chapter after chapter' Christopher Price, *New Statesman*

Cultural Action for Freedom

Paulo Freire

Paulo Freire's *Cultural Action for Freedom* is the educational process itself, and, particularly and crucially, teaching literacy to adults. Within his definition of that process learners assume from the beginning the role of creative subjects. Learning is not a matter of memorizing and repeating given words, syllables and phrases, but rather of reflecting critically on the process of reading and writing itself and on the profound significance of language. As the most important vehicle of cultural transmission language, and therefore literacy, must be used, developed and given meaning by those whose will it must express.

In seeking to challenge the conceptual and cultural domination that prevailed in the slums and villages of Latin America, Freire developed a highly original and spectacularly successful method of teaching literacy. In this book he outlines the principles which underlay that method and their implications.

Pedogogy of the Oppressed

Paulo Freire

In Paulo Freire's hands literacy is a weapon for social change.
Education once again becomes the means by which men
can perceive, interpret, criticize and finally transform the
world about them.

Freire's attack on the 'culture of silence' inhabited by the vast
numbers of illiterate peasants in Brazil's poorest areas has
contributed in an extraordinary way to the development of a
sense of purpose and identity among the oppressed and
demoralized majority. His work is the result of a process of
reflection in the midst of a struggle to create a new social order. His
is the authentic voice of the Third World, but his methodology
and philosophy are also important in the industrialized countries
where a new culture of silence threatens to dominate an
overconsuming and overmanaged population, where education too
often means merely socialization. In contrast, Freire's approach
concentrates upon the ability to deal creatively with reality.